CHAMPIONSHIP '93

CHAMPIONSHIP '96

THE EUROPEAN FOOTBALL CHAMPIONSHIPS 1996

Glen Phillips & Tim Oldham

BOXTREE

First published in Great Britain in 1996 by Boxtree Limited

1 2 3 4 5 6 7 8 9 10

Designed by Nigel Davies
Printed and bound in Great Britain by Cox and Wyman Ltd.,
Reading, Berkshire for:

Boxtree Limited
Broadwall House
21 Broadwall
London   SE1 9PL

A CIP catalogue entry for this book is available from the
British Library.

ISBN   07522 1031 9

Front cover photograph courtesy of AllSport

CONTENTS

INTRODUCTION

The greatest sporting event to hit England since the 1966 World Cup will kick off at 3.00 pm on 8 June 1996 at Wembley Stadium, when England and Switzerland play the opening game in the tenth European Championship. The match will herald the start of a three-week festival of football, featuring the sixteen best teams in Europe, to decide which country will succeed Denmark as champions.

The European Championship is now second in importance only to the World Cup and is just as tough a competition to win. The tournament has been expanded to sixteen competing teams for the first time, and among the unique guest list are all eight previous winners (although the Soviet Union is now represented by Russia and Czechoslovakia by the Czech Republic). Russia, Croatia and the Czech Republic all qualified at their first attempt. The only notable absentees are Sweden and Belgium. The strength of the competition and of European football is illustrated by the fact that six of the eight World Cup quarter-finalists are here.

Since the rather defensive and unambitious style in the 1992 European Championship there has been a move towards brighter, more expansive football encouraged by the likes of Ajax and national teams such as Portugal, Holland, Croatia and Romania. And with some of the finest players in the world on display – Baggio, Rui Costa, Hagi, Stoichkov, Klinsmann, Shearer, Bergkamp and Boban, to name but a few, the tournament promises to be an outstanding feast of football.

There will be no easy games. The group stage will require three consistently high-level performances over nine days or so before the top two from each group qualify for the quarter-finals. From here on in it will be straight knock-out, and if any games are drawn at the end of ninety minutes, the first goal scored in the thirty minute extra-time period will decide the game under the new 'golden goal' rule. If this fails to produce a winner, the tie will go to penalties.

The pressure to succeed on each team will be immense, but on none more so, one suspects, than England. Playing at home in front of your own supporters can be a big advantage, but the weight of expectation can prove too heavy – indeed, the record of host nations has not been good in recent tournaments. Whatever the outcome, it is going to be a memorable championship and we hope that this book will enhance your enjoyment of the event. It contains a comprehensive history of the tournament, from the inaugural competition in 1960 to the present day, and profiles each of the sixteen teams particpating in 1996: how they qualified, who the key players are and how each country has fared in previous championships. There's a complete schedule of matches, venues and a fill-in guide to enable you to complete your own record of the tournament. Finally, there is a fun look at which players would grace a select all-time European Championship team. Everyone will have his or her own opinion: see if you agree with the selection.

THE TEERMS

Group A

England, Switzerland, Holland, Scotland

The pattern of games for Group A has given England, the seeded team, an excellent chance of progressing to the second round, but whether it will be as group winners or runners-up will probably depend on their final match. Although the opening contests are often tense affairs, Switzerland are ideal first opponents and England should look at this encounter as their best chance of winning a game. They comfortably beat an admittedly weakened Swiss side back in November, which should give them the necessary confidence. The Swiss dismissed that result as an irrelevance, but doubts over the fitness of key players and the loss of inspirational coach Roy Hodgson could prove a tough hurdle to overcome.

One week later, England face Scotland in what will undoubtedly be a passionate revival of the world's oldest fixture. Scotland are likely to be looking for their first points – not that they will require any additional motivation, as beating England will be seen as just as important as Scotland getting through themselves. With so much pride at stake the game is unlikely be a classic in terms of flowing, cultured football, but this could be the time for Alan Shearer to make his mark (he will probably be trying at the same time to beat club-mate Colin Hendry, who will be in the middle of the Scottish defense).

England's final match, against Holland, should decide who wins the group and could provide an intriguing clash between Arsenal team-mates David Seaman and Dennis Bergkamp. Recent games between the two teams have favoured the Dutch. In 1993, Holland beat England

2-0 in Rotterdam after a 2-2 draw at Wembley to qualify for the World Cup, and Marco van Basten's hat-trick in 1988 effectively put Bobby Robson's men out of the European Championship.Against that record, England held the Dutch 0-0 in Cagliari in the 1990 World Cup.

England and Holland, then, should be the two qualifiers, but underdog status has traditionally appealed to the Scots' psyche and they will never be more fired up than in the game against England at Wembley.

England v Switzerland	8 June, 3.00 pm, Wembley	**ITV**
Holland v Scotland	10 June, 4.30 pm, Villa Park	**ITV**
Switzerland v Holland	13 June, 7.30 pm, Villa Park	**BBC**
England v Scotland	15 June, 3.00 pm, Wembley	**BBC**
Scotland v Switzerland	18 June, 7.30 pm, Villa Park	**ITV**
England v Holland	18 June, 7.30 pm, Wembley	**ITV**

England

Strip:
White shirts, dark blue shorts, white socks
Change:
All claret with dark blue trim

Coach:
Terry Venables

FIFA world ranking:
24

It has been twelve years since a host country won the championship but Terry Venables and his players are aiming to reverse this trend. Being hosts can work both for and against you – it worked against Italy in the 1990 World Cup, as the further they progressed the more nervous they seemed to become. However, there is little doubt that the possibility of playing every game at Wembley will be a massive advantage for England's national team.

While the rest of Europe has been battling it out for the coveted fifteen places in the finals, Venables has been engaged in assessing the squad which will carry England's dreams of European Championship success. He has tried out a number of new players and the introduction of Teddy Sheringham, Gary Neville, Steve Stone and Jamie Redknapp, among others, has vindicated this policy. After a relatively trouble-free start, Venables' selection and tactics did come in for some criticism, but he would do well to remember that the two most fiercely criticized coaches in the 1994 World Cup were Italy's Arrigo Sacchi and Brazil's Carlos Alberto Parreira, the coaches of the two finalists.

The defence has changed little since Venables took over in 1994, with David Seaman and Tim Flowers being given the opportunity to claim the number 1 jersey. But even though both can be brilliant on their day, neither has really done enough to be declared outright first-choice goalkeeper. Seaman probably has the edge.

The back four is based around the solid and experienced figures of Gary Pallister and Tony Adams, who have played many times together and built up a good partnership. Graeme le Saux would have been the first choice left back, but he suffered serious ankle damage in Blackburn's game against Middlesbrough in December, which has effectively ruled him out of contention. His place will most likely be taken by Stuart Pearce, who may lack a yard in pace these days but is nevertheless an experienced international who links well with attacks and takes a pretty mean free kick.

One of the most promising newcomers to the squad is Manchester United's Gary Neville at full back. Still only twenty-one, his rise from the United youth team to England international has been of meteoric proportions but there is no doubt that he has fitted in confidently.

At the start of Venables' tenure the England midfield was pretty much the preserve of David Platt, Paul Ince and Paul Gascoigne, but these veterans have come under increasing pressure from a crop of talented youngsters. Steve McManaman, Steve Stone, Nick Barmby and Jamie Redknapp have all been given their chance by Venables and they have acquitted themselves well.

Ince was the first to suffer when he pulled out of the Umbro Cup last summer. Venables was not happy at his decision, and he has not selected the Inter midfielder since. This opened the door for Redknapp, who won his first cap against Colombia on the strength of his highly influential and creative role at Liverpool. He may lack Ince's defensive ability and tackling prowess, but he more than makes up for it in his passing, vision and touch. After a slow start in Italian football, Ince has now evolved into the same dynamic, thrusting force for Inter as he was for Manchester United, which can only be good news for England.

Once the first name on the team sheet, David Platt has suffered a series of injuries and in January was admitted for a second operation on his left knee in five months. The first had been to repair a cartilage and the second was necessary when floating cartilage was revealed. Platt's great strength is his fantastic goal-scoring record – twenty-six in fifty-five games – but although no one works harder in midfield, he does need someone to take over the duties of marshalling the midfield and defence to allow him to make those penetrative runs into the box.

Gascoigne has treated us to his full range of talents only in tantalizingly brief spells and he is another player seemingly beset by niggling injuries. Doubts are growing about his effectiveness and stamina and, as hard as it is to come to terms with, the best of the virtuoso who entranced us with his skill in Italia '90 may be behind him. But he still possesses skills other players can only dream about. His wonderful ball control and accurate passing are still there for all to see but those explosive spurts which would propel him deep into the heart of the opponents' area are becoming less frequent. Yet Gascoigne remains the one player who can seriously be described as a genius and this is as good a stage as any on which he can prove it.

Jamie Redknapp would appear to be the most able successor to Gazza, and indeed he formed a good partnership with the Rangers midfielder against Colombia. However, it was unfortunate for Redknapp that an injury early in the friendly against Switzerland provided Steve Stone with his big chance. As a substitute against Norway, Stone had added life to England's turgid attack with his consistently accurate centres. Now, given virtually an entire match to establish himself, he produced more high-quality service for Shearer and Sheringham, and gave England much-needed width. More of a wide midfielder than an out-and-out winger, he capped a brilliant performance by scoring the third goal.

Stone's success is in contrast to that of McManaman. The twenty-four-year-old Liverpool winger has shown glimpses of his potential, but has been less effective in the fixed role on the left. He probably needs a freer role, but can England afford to grant him this?

Robert Lee's fine form for Newcastle United has also enhanced Venables' midfield options, but it seems that perhaps the most gifted player in England, Matt le Tissier, is destined not to play a role in the team unless there is a massive about-turn in the coach's approach. Half the country believe Le Tissier is the most brilliant thing since Coco Pops; the other half think he's too laid back. When he has been brought on as a substitute he has struggled to adapt to the pace of the game but he should be given a real opportunity.

The remaining piece in the midfield jigsaw is Darren Anderton, who has been recovering from a hernia problem. Anderton made his England debut against Denmark in March 1994, since when he has been prepared to take on defenders and put in telling crosses in a style England fans have not seen for some time. Anderton has pace, versatility and stamina (he was a schoolboy cross-country champion) and with two good feet, he could play in the same team as Stone.

Alan Shearer looks certain to be England's first-choice striker and after an encouraging performance against Switzerland, Teddy Sheringham would appear to be the player best suited to be his partner – if Venables decides there is to be a partner, that is. Sheringham gave Shearer the support he has been desperate for and the partnership is clearly worth continuing. Sheringham will also drop deep and link the play, and he creates chances for others as well as scoring plenty of goals himself. Blackburn's poor start to the season didn't seem to affect Shearer's appetite for scoring goals in the Premiership, but he failed to make any impression against Champions League opposition, the sort of defences he will face in June. Shearer hasn't scored for England since bagging two against the United States in September 1994, but it's hard to believe that a player of his class, who can score from tap-ins or 30-yard drives, will not end the barren spell soon. And where better place to do so than in the forthcoming finals?

Les Ferdinand has been in brilliant form for Newcastle United but despite a good performance alongside Shearer against the Portuguese, he is perhaps too similar to Shearer to form an effective partnership. Ferdinand would probably prefer to line up as the out-and-out striker. Sheringham lacks the acceleration of Ferdinand, but there is more subtlety to his game. He's a clever, flexible striker capable of playing as the principal or support. Against Switzerland, he scored with a stunning header from Stone's cross and linked the play with some deft touches. His distribution and passing have improved and he looks like a genuine international.

However, Liverpool's Robbie Fowler must get a look-in at some stage. He is matching Shearer's goalscoring in the Premiership and has developed an almost telepathic understanding with Stan Collymore. Perhaps this partnership should be given an airing.

Against Colombia and Switzerland there were encouraging signs that things were coming together. In the Switzerland game the players grew in confidence as the match progressed and the goals went in. England had the self-assurance to probe for openings and not simply hoof the ball upfield. In the build-up to Sheringham's goal, for example, England looked for an opening on the left then switched to the right rather than forcing the pass and losing it. Stone's measured cross and Sheringham's head rewarded the patient and well-worked approach work.

On reflection, a draw against Norway in Oslo was not a bad

result, just a drab one. And against Portugal, Venables proved that the squad has sufficient depth to allow him to adapt his team to compensate for late injuries. That ability will be important in the finals. England held an admittedly under-strength Portuguese side and although they were outpaced and out-thought at times, they were never really outclassed.

Each of England's group opponents will pose a different problem. Remembering how they lost their opening match to a fired-up Republic of Ireland in the 1988 finals, it might be just as well that they are not encountering the passionate Scots until 15 June. Switzerland are one of England's recent victims and Holland are probably best saved for last.

England qualified as hosts

PAST PERFORMANCE IN EUROPEAN CHAMPIONSHIP FINALS

Best performance: Third place, 1968

England didn't enter the inaugural Nations Cup and their first taste of the championship was in the 1964 series, when they lost 6-3 on aggregate to France in the first round. England's best showing was in 1968, when they beat the Soviet Union in the third-place match.

In 1972, England lost in the quarter-finals to eventual winners West Germany. They failed to qualify in 1976 and lost out to Belgium and Italy in the 1980 finals.

In 1984, England had the misfortune to be drawn against the brilliant Danes in qualifying Group 3. Hopes were high in 1988 after an impressive qualification which included a 4-1 win over Yugoslavia, but England then proceeded to lose all their group matches, the nadir being the stunning 3-1 defeat at the hands of Dutch striker Marco van Basten. England went into the 1992 finals as one of the favourites, only for two goalless draws, followed by a drubbing by the rampant home nation, to book them seats on the early plane home once again.

1960: Did not enter
1964: First round
England 1 France 1; France 5 England 2.
1968: Third place
Quarter-final: England 1 Spain 0; Spain 1 England 2.
Semi-final: Yugoslavia 1 England 0.
Third-place play-off: England 2 Soviet Union 0.
1972: Quarter-finalists
England 1 West Germany 3; West Germany 0 England 0
1976: Eliminated in qualifying tournament
1980: First round
Group Two: Belgium 1 England 1; Italy 1 England 0;
England 2 Spain 1.
1984: Eliminated in qualifying tournament
1988: First round
Group Two: Republic of Ireland 1 England 0;
Holland 3 England 1; Soviet Union 3 England 1.
1992: First round
Group One: Denmark 0 England 0; France 0 England 0;
Sweden 2 England 1.

Switzerland

Strip:
Red shirts, white shorts, red socks
Change:
All white with red trim

Coach:
Artur Jorge

FIFA World ranking:
20

Until Englishman Roy Hodgson took over as national coach in 1992, football had never figured prominently on the Swiss list of popular sports and the national team hadn't experienced any success of sufficient note to improve its standing in the national psyche. However, under Hodgson's guidance they improved steadily, became more consistent and better organized, and reached the finals of a major tournament for the first time since 1966 when they qualified for the 1994 World Cup.

The team that travelled to the States was undoubtedly the most experienced the Swiss had ever fielded, and after a 1-1 draw against the hosts, they produced a performance which had the cowbells ringing around the stadium when they beat Romania 4-1. Despite then losing to Colombia, the Swiss qualified for the second round, where they were knocked out by Spain.

Hodgson became a national hero and continued Switzerland's excellent progress with qualification for Euro '96. The Swiss made a cracking start to their campaign, beating fancied Sweden (4-2) and Iceland, and even managing a 2-1 win away in the pressure-cooker atmosphere of Istanbul against Turkey. Swiss striker Kubilay Turkyilmaz, who then played his club football for Galatasaray, was left out of this game at his own request, for fear of reprisals if he contributed in any way to Swiss success in his parents' homeland and in front of his own club supporters.

And indeed, Group 3 quickly developed into a two-horse race

between Switzerland and Turkey. The Swiss battled well to save a point against Hungary, despite being without the injured Stephane Chapuisat, Adrian Knup and Turkyilmaz again, but then lost to Turkey in the return tie. However, a 3-0 victory over Hungary in October made sure that the Swiss were one of the first teams to qualify. After this performance, one Swiss TV commentor even went so far as to describe Hodgson as the greatest man in the history of Swiss sport. Honour indeed.

Having achieved wonders with the national team, in October 1995 Hodgson accepted an offer from Italian giants Internazionale to join them as a coach. It was a mark of how highly they respected his services that Inter suggested they would be willing to allow him to continue in an advisory role for the Swiss. However, three months into Hodgson's new job the Swiss FA decided that he couldn't really be expected to devote enough of his energies to the national team and appointed Portuguese coach Artur Jorge. Jorge had recently been dismissed from his position at Benfica following a revolt by the fans, but he is a respected coach in Europe. If skill at languages alone was the recipe for success, he may as well make room in the trophy cabinet now: he speaks German, Italian, French, English and Spanish as well as his native Portuguese.

Although they rely on a strong all-round team performance, the Swiss can only really boast two players of outstanding ability. Although he looks as if he could win the world squinting championships, Stephane Chapuisat is a world-class striker who plays his club football for 1995 Bundesliga champions, Borussia Dortmund. He is a prolific goalscorer for club and country and has formed a good understanding with his tall striking partner, Adrian Knup. However, a cruciate ligament injury has seriously jeopardized Chapuisat's chances and much will depend on how quickly he recovers. He would be a major loss to the side.

Another key member is Ciriaco Sforza, who also plays in the German Bundesliga for Bayern Munich. The twenty-six-year-old central midfielder directs much of the play from the middle, creating attacking options for himself and his strikers. In the friendly against England, he was instrumental in many of Switzerland's attacks, releasing the pace of Alain Sutter, Turkyilmaz and Knup, whose neat near-post header gave Switzerland the lead.

With his long blonde hair, it's difficult to miss Sutter. The ponytailed midfielder had a magnificent World Cup scoring a tremendous goal against Romania in Switzerland's best performance of the finals. He missed the second-round defeat against Spain with a toe injury and his powerful running and passing were sorely missed. Since then he has had an unhappy spell at Bayern Munich, where he struggled to keep his place in a team which was packed with world-class players, and moved to FC Freiburg in the summer.

Sutter is an intelligent player and one who is also prepared to air his opinions. Just before the start of the second qualifying game against Sweden, Sutter and several team-mates unfurled a banner which read 'Stop It Chirac', a comment on France's resumption of nuclear testing in the South Pacific. The gesture was warmly received by the crowd but less so by the Swiss FA, who had not been notified of the proposed demonstration.

The Swiss were without a number of their first-team players in their 3-1 defeat by England at Wembley and played like a team who were not prepared to risk picking up unnecessary injuries. After a tight first half they started to give England the time and space to play and were punished in the second half. They will be a different proposition in June as long as Jorge can emulate the motivational abilities of his predecessor.

HOW THEY QUALIFIED

GROUP THREE	P	W	D	L	F	A	PTS
Switzerland	8	5	2	1	15	7	17
Turkey	8	4	3	1	16	8	15
Sweden	8	2	3	3	9	10	9
Hungary	8	2	2	4	7	13	8
Iceland	8	1	2	5	3	12	5

Iceland 0 Sweden 1; Hungary 2 Turkey 2; Turkey 5 Iceland 0;
Switzerland 4 Sweden 2; **Switzerland 1** Iceland 0;
Sweden 2 Hungary 0; Turkey 1 **Switzerland 2**; Turkey 2 Sweden 1;
Hungary 2 **Switzerland 2**; Hungary 1 Sweden 0;
Switzerland 1 Turkey 2; Sweden 1 Iceland 1; Iceland 2 Hungary 1;
Iceland 0 **Switzerland 2**; Sweden 0 **Switzerland 0**;
Turkey 2 Hungary 0; **Switzerland 3** Hungary 0; Iceland 0 Turkey 0;
Hungary 1 Iceland 0; Sweden 2 Turkey 2.

PAST PERFORMANCE IN EUROPEAN CHAMPIONSHIP FINALS

Best performance: First round 1964

Switzerland gave their most notable performances in international football when they hosted the 1954 World Cup. They beat Italy twice to reach the quarter-finals but were then defeated in an extraordinary match against Austria – 3-0 up after twenty-three minutes, they eventually lost 7-5. Reaching the second round in the 1994 World Cup was a tremendous achievement, but prior to the current finals, the nearest Switzerland have come to qualifying for the European Championship finals was in 1972, when they finished second to England in their qualifying group.

1960: **Did not enter**
1964: **First round**
Holland 3 Switzerland 1; Switzerland 1 Holland 1.
1968-92: **Eliminated in qualifying round.**

Holland

Strip:
Orange shirts, white shorts, orange socks
Change:
White shirts, orange shorts, white socks

Manager:
Guus Hiddink

FIFA World ranking:
6

Following their superb performance in the final-place deciding game against the Republic of Ireland, Holland were immediately installed as favourites for the championship. Based on that display, few people would disagree that the Dutch possess a supremely gifted team which could repeat the success of the 1988 championship-winning side of Ruud Gullit, Marco van Basten and Frank Rijkaard, but it should be remembered that no matter how good the team looked that December night at Anfield, they had managed to get themselves into the precarious position of having to contest the play-off in the first place with a series of less spectacular performances. During qualification they had dropped four points to group winners the Czech Republic, and needed to win their last game against Norway to earn the play-off against Ireland.

After Holland secured their place in the finals, manager Guus Hiddink tempered the glowing reports heaped on his team by reminding anyone who cared to listen of their ignominious 1-0 defeat at the hands of Belarus – hardly one of Europe's footballing giants. Holland were dismal that night, despite their seven Ajax players, and with three games remaining it looked as if they would be watching the European Championship from their living rooms.

The Dutch went on to beat Belarus in the return tie and Marc Overmars scored a hat-trick against Malta to take them to within three points of Norway. The two teams met for the showdown in Rotterdam and in one of their most impressive performances the

Dutch fought hard for the victory they needed. The visitors had just one objective in mind – the one point that would secure their own qualification – and they weathered Dutch pressure in the first half. There was an element of luck in Clarence Seedorf's opening goal, which ballooned over the Norwegian keeper, Frode Grodaas. At 1-0 down Norway had to take risks, and they came close to equalising before Holland added two more in the final two minutes. The result meant that both teams ended level on points, though Holland had the better record of the games between the two sides.

Still, the Dutch do look as if they are coming good at the right time. Since their less than spectacular World Cup – enlivened only by an entertaining 3-2 defeat at the hands of Brazil – Hiddink has developed a good atmosphere among the players, and they are performing more and more as a team. This shouldn't really come as a surprise since most of them come from Ajax, but at national level the Dutch game has been frequently hindered by dissent between the players and the manager, a situation which certainly undermined their progress in the 1994 World Cup under Dick Advocaat. In fact, the Dutch transformation came about through the adoption of the Ajax style by Hiddink. His players are obviously more comfortable with the tactics and approach that have brought them European and world club success.

It is almost impossible to look at any of the great Dutch players over the past four decades without seeing the influence of Ajax in their playing history. And the prescence of eight players from the club in the team that destroyed the Republic of Ireland mean that Ajax will be just as influential among the current team as it was in the early seventies. Then, with the inspiration of Johan Cruyff, Ajax won the European Cup from 1971 to 1973, playing their trademark total football, and it was Cruyff, as manager, who took them to further European club success in 1987.

Despite the fact that they continue to sell many of their best players, there always seems to be another highly talented youngster capable of stepping into the Ajax team, thanks to their world-renowned youth scheme. When the 'irreplaceable' Marco van Basten left to join Milan, Dennis Bergkamp replaced him. After Bergkamp came Patrick Kluivert. And the process continues.

Total football remains Holland's objective on the field. Although the team lines up in what can best be described as 4-3-3, they can switch this around at any time within their completely flexible and fluid system. Edwin van der Sar is developing as a top goalkeeper, while the defence is built on Michael Reiziger on the right, Winston Bogarde on the left with Frank de Boer and Danny Blind as the flexible, central-defensive playmakers.

Formerly with Ajax and now with Sampdoria, nineteen-year-old Clarence Seedorf, Holland's top scorer in the qualifiers, is joined in midfield by Edgar Davids with either the skilful Richard Witschge or Ronald de Boer, who operates as a right-sided attacking midfielder. Up front, Kluivert spearheads the attack, partnered by Bergkamp, and, until recently, Marc Overmars. Sadly, Overmars has been ruled out of the championship after exploratory knee surgery revealed serious ligament damage to his left knee. It's a major blow to the team – Overmars' pace on the left flank stretched even the most mobile defender as he created chances for himself or Kluivert. The Dutch could be faced with a double whammy: Kluiverts is awaiting prosecution for causing death by dangerous driving in a car accident in September 1995, and could face a possible jail sentence.

Despite their youth, the Dutch team are very experienced against international opposition, courtesy again of Ajax's success in the Champions League and World Club Cup. Against Real Madrid in the Champions League, for example, Ajax couldn't have tested the cross-bar more if they'd asked it questions on astrophysics and the final score of 2-0 didn't by any stretch of the imagination reflect their dominanace. But even though they didn't score until the second half, they never looked anything other than confident of winning. The same can be said of the game against the Irish who have been the undoing of some technically superior sides in the past. For most of the match the Dutch looked calm and composed and prepared to work and to wait for the inevitable opening.

This is all rather a daunting prospect for their Group A opponents. Manager Guus Hiddink believes it is a good draw for the Dutch as it will allow them to play in their favoured way. He sees their third game against England at Wembley as the toughest one.

HOW THEY QUALIFIED

GROUP FIVE	P	W	D	L	F	A	PTS
Czech Rep	10	6	3	1	21	6	21
Holland	10	6	2	2	23	5	20
Norway	10	6	2	2	17	7	20
Belarus	10	3	2	5	8	13	11
Luxembourg	10	3	1	6	3	21	10
Malta	10	0	2	8	2	22	2

Czech Republic 6 Malta 1; Luxembourg 0 **Holland 4**; Norway 1
Belarus 0; Malta 0 Czech Republic 0; Belarus 2 Luxembourg 0; Norway 1
Holland 1; Belarus 0 Norway 4; **Holland 0** Czech Republic 0;
Malta 0 Norway 1; **Holland 5** Luxembourg 0; Malta 0 Luxembourg 0;
Czech Republic 4 Belarus 2; Luxembourg 0 Norway 2; **Holland 4**
Malta 0; Belarus 1 Malta 1; Czech Republic 3 **Holland 1**; Norway 5
Luxembourg 0; Belarus 1 **Holland 0**; Luxembourg 1 Czech Republic 0;
Norway 2 Malta 0; Norway 1 Czech Republic 1; Czech Republic 2
Norway 0; Luxembourg 1 Malta 0; **Holland 1** Belarus 0; Belarus 0
Czech Republic 2; Malta 0 **Holland 4**; Luxembourg 0 Belarus 0; Malta
0 Belarus 2; Czech Republic 3 Luxembourg 0; **Holland 3** Norway 0.

Play-off: Holland 2 - 0 Republic of Ireland

PAST PERFORMANCE IN EUROPEAN CHAMPIONSHIP FINALS

Best performance: Winners, 1988

If ever a team deserved to win a major international title in the seventies, it was the Dutch. Twice they were runners-up to the hosts in consecutive World Cup finals, and in between they lost to a talented Czech team in the semi-finals of the 1976 European Championship. Their only consolation was that Czechoslovakia beat arch-rivals West Germany in the final. After so much success, the Dutch national side went through a lean period in the early eighties, failing to qualify for the 1982 and 1986 World Cup finals and the 1984 European Championship.

However, a revival was just around the corner. Ajax won their first European trophy for fourteen years, the Cup-Winners' Cup in 1987, and PSV Eindhoven won the European Cup the following year. In the 1988 European Championship, the Milan-based trio of Van Basten, Gullit and Rijkaard led the national side to their first international success, beating West Germany and the Soviet Union along the way, with a series of performances reminiscent of the golden days of Dutch football.

1960: Did not enter

1964: Second round
> First round: Holland 3 Switzerland 1;
> Switzerland 1 Holland 1.
> Second round: Holland 1 Luxembourg 1;
> Luxembourg 2 Holland 1.

1968: Eliminated in qualifying tournament

1972: Eliminated in qualifying tournament

1976: Third place
> Quarter-final: Holland 5 Belgium 0; Belgium 1 Holland 2.
> Semi-final: Czechoslovakia 3 Holland 1 (aet).
> Third-place play-off: Holland 3 Yugoslavia 2 (aet).

1980: First round
> Group One: Holland 1 Greece 0;
> West Germany 3 Holland 2; Czechoslovakia 1 Holland 1.

1984: Eliminated in qualifying tournament

1988: Winners
> Group Two: Soviet Union 1 Holland 0; Holland 3 England 1;
> Holland 1 Republic of Ireland 0.
> Semi-final: Holland 2 West Germany 1.
> Final: Holland 2 Soviet Union 0.

1992: Semi-finalists
> Group Two: Holland 1 Scotland 0; Holland 0 CIS 0;
> Holland 3 Germany 1.
> Semi-final: Denmark 2 Holland 2 (5-4 pens).

Scotland

Strip:
All dark blue
Change:
All white with dark blue trim

Manager:
Craig Brown

FIFA World ranking:
26

Craig Brown can look back over a tricky but pleasing qualification. Any team that can draw at home and away with Russia deserves credit, and Scotland's points tally was bettered only by Germany, Spain and, of course, Russia. The group was not one of the strongest but once in the finals Scotland are more than capable of matching anyone in terms of teamwork and spirit.

What's more, the famous Tartan Army will be on the move south again, thanks to the quirk of fate which has placed the Scots in the same group as England, thereby reviving the oldest fixture in world football. Scotland will come face to face with England at Wembley on 15 June, having last met at Hampden Park in 1989 when Bobby Robson's team won 2-0. Their last appearance at Wembley also ended in defeat, to a Peter Beardsley goal.

Scotland have a proud tradition in the World Cup, where they have played in five of the last six finals, and this will be their second appearance in the European Championship finals. They did well in the 1992 Championship, although they have never progressed beyond the first round in either major tournament. They may never have a better chance than the one they have this time round.

Craig Brown took over as team manager after Scotland's disappointing bid to reach the World Cup finals in 1994 and he deserves credit for maximizing relatively limited resources. The team might not have been sparkling, but they have been efficient and particularly mean in defence.

The Scots began their quest for the championship with a trip to Helsinki for a testing game against Finland, who had Ajax's brilliant striker Jari Litmanen in the front line. Not only did the Scottish defence prevent Litmanen from scoring, but they also kept out the rest of the Finnish attack with some excellent defending – a trend they would maintain throughout their campaign. Goals from Duncan Shearer and Celtic's John Collins gave them a very useful start.

In the next game, at home to the Faroe Isles, an all-important early goal after four minutes by Bolton's John McGinley set Scotland on the road to a comfortable 5-1 win. Against group favourites Russia at home, they did well to earn a 1-1 draw. Moving on to Greece they knew they needed to come away with a result. Scotland soaked up the inevitable pressure but were undone by two controversial penalty decisions from the Dutch referee. The first was to award the penalty kick from which Apostolakis scored the only goal of the game; the second was to deny the Scots the opportunity to equalize when the visitors claimed that John Spencer had been tripped up.

After all the Scots' good work this defeat was potentially damaging and left Greece at the head of the group with maximum points. Although Scotland were lying second, the Russians were only three points behind them with two games in hand and were clear favourites to win the group. In light of this situation, Scotland could not afford to lose in Russia and they produced one of their most resolute displays to come away with a point from a 0-0 draw. In defence, Colin Hendry was magnificent and Jim Leighton, with a string of fine saves, thwarted one of the most dangerous attacks in Europe, which was to brush every other Group 8 team aside.

Successive away wins over San Marino and the Faroe Isles, both by 2-0, put Scotland into third place behind Russia and new leaders Finland, who had beaten Greece (still a close fourth). With three games remaining, all at home, qualification was within Scotland's grasp. First up was the crucial return tie against Greece. On a warm August evening, a marvellous headed goal from substitute Ally McCoist was enough to beat the Greeks and the news that Russia had thrashed Finland 6-0 away rounded off a thoroughly satisfying evening.

The last major hurdle was overcome with a workmanlike 1-0 victory over Finland, thanks to Scott Booth's tenth minute goal which put the Scots joint top with Russia, who still had a game in hand. More importantly, Scotland were now five points clear of Greece in third place and their spot in England was all but mathematically guaranteed, pending UEFA's complicated calculations to decide the best runners-up. Shortly before their final game against San Marino, results elsewhere confirmed that Scotland would take one of the six best runners-up spots, and they celebrated with an easy 5-1 win.

Scotland's strength is their defence. The two Colins, Calderwood and Hendry, may not be the most skilled central defenders in the competition but no others will match them for do-or-die commitment. One of the most remarkable aspects of their qualification has been Jim Leighton's return to international action, first as back-up to Andy Goram, then as first-choice goalkeeper himself. He appears to have fully regained his confidence and at this rate he could make jokes about Scottish goalkeepers a thing of the past, appreciated only by those old enough to remember Alan Rough.

The heart of the team lies in midfield, where Gary McAllister and John Collins have provided the creativity, inspiration and aggression to carry Scotland through. Collins was also Scotland's top scorer and his ability to finish as well as to create is an element of his game for which Scotland have been thankful in the absence of a proven goalscorer. Collins' energetic running combined with McAllister's leadership, drive and great distribution will be crucial factors for the side.

Injuries have prevented Craig Brown from fielding a regular partnership in attack, and he has used practically every striker available. Booth is now one of the first choice forwards, paired with his Aberdeen team-mate Eoin Jess, but Brown's options have been widened with the return of the experienced goal-getters Ally McCoist and Duncan Ferguson of Everton.

Scotland have a resilient, competent side, but one feels they lack the touch and vision of a truly world-class player such as a Denis Law or Kenny Dalglish. However, the role of underdog has traditionally appealed to the Scots. If Brown can harness greater attacking threat to what is a strong midfield and at the same time maintain the new-found defensive solidity, ambition need not be seen as fanciful.

HOW THEY QUALIFIED

GROUP EIGHT	P	W	D	L	F	A	PTS
Russia	10	8	2	0	34	5	26
Scotland	10	7	2	1	19	3	23
Greece	10	6	0	4	23	9	18
Finland	10	5	0	5	18	18	15
Faroe Isles	10	2	0	8	10	35	6
San Marino	10	0	0	10	2	36	0

Finland 0 **Scotland 2**; Faroe Isles 1 Greece 5; **Scotland 5** Faroe Isles 1; Greece 4 Finland 0; Russia 4 San Marino 0; **Scotland 1** Russia 1; Greece 2 San Marino 0; Finland 5 Faroe Isles 0; Finland 4 San Marino 1; Greece 1 **Scotland 0**; Russia 0 **Scotland 0**; San Marino 0 Finland 2; San Marino 0 **Scotland 2**; Greece 0 Russia 3; Faroe Isles 0 Finland 4; Russia 3 Faroe Isles 0; Faroe Isles 3 San Marino 0; Faroe Isles 0 **Scotland 2**; San Marino 0 Russia 7; Finland 2 Greece 1; **Scotland 1** Greece 0; Finland 0 Russia 6; **Scotland 1** Finland 0; Faroe Isles 2 Russia 5; San Marino 0 Greece 4; Russia 2 Greece 1; San Marino 1 Faroe Isles 3; **Scotland 5** San Marino 0; Russia 3 Finland 1; Greece 5 Faroe Isles 0.

PAST PERFORMANCE IN EUROPEAN CHAMPIONSHIP FINALS

Best performance: First round 1992

Despite a fine record in qualifying for the World Cup, the Scots had never qualified for the European Championship prior to 1992. The closest they had come was in 1968, when their Group 8 clashes with England went down to the wire. The largest crowd ever at a European Championship match, 132,000, crammed into Hampden Park, where Scotland needed to win to go through. England held them to a 1-1 draw and progressed themselves.

In 1987 a last-gasp 1-0 victory over Bulgaria in Sofia helped Scotland's Group 7 rivals the Republic of Ireland through to the finals the following year.

In 1992, Scotland qualified from a tough group and although they lost to Holland and Germany in the finals they refused to be overwhelmed and played well. Somewhat surprisingly, Scotland beat the CIS, who had posed such problems for the Dutch and Germans.

1960-64: **Did not enter**
1968-88: **Eliminated in qualifying tournament**
1992:   **First round**
             Holland 1 Scotland 0; Germany 2 Scotland 0;
             Scotland 3 CIS 0.

Group B

Spain, Bulgaria, Romania, France

This is probably the most evenly matched group of the four and contains one of the highlights of the finals: Hristo Stoichkov versus Gheorghe Hagi. However, Spain are the seeded team of the group and are an improved and stronger outfit since they lost to Italy in the quarter-finals of the 1994 World Cup. The Spanish team will know plenty about the capabilities of many of their Bulgarian and Romanian opponents as they play alongside and against such men as Hagi, Florin Raducioiu and Luboslav Penev week in, week out. The inside information will not necessarily make containing the likes of Hagi any easier, but Spain are enjoying a good run of form and appear to have the consistency to string three strong group games together. Their one difficulty may lie against France. Since Spain lost to France in the 1984 European Championship final, the two teams have met three times, with France emerging victorious in each.

In fact, France may hold the key to the group. They were very difficult to beat in the qualifying rounds but, at times, found it correspondingly difficult to beat anyone else. Their best performance was the 3-1 victory over Romania in Bucharest but they followed that up with a less convincing win over Israel. Group games in these finals are all about putting in three good performances in the space of eight or nine days. Three draws is not going to be good enough.

French coach Aimé Jacquet's decision as to whether or not to play British favourites David Ginola – at his home ground – and Eric Cantona will be eagerly anticipated. Although they will find Romania dangerous on the counter-attack, the French defence is now one of the most frugal in Europe and it will take all of Hagi's brilliance to create an opening. Bulgaria have been something of a *bête noire* for France, most recently in their last-minute win in Paris, which saw them qualify for the 1994 World Cup at the expense of the French. This time round France will not be so profligate in defence, but it is another game which could swing either way.

It's almost too tight a group to call but, if pushed, we'd plump for Bulgaria to join Spain in the quarter-finals.

Spain v Bulgaria	9 June, 2.30, Elland Road	**ITV**
Romania v France	10 June, 7.30 pm, St James's Park	**BBC**
Bulgaria v Romania	13 June, 4.30 pm, St James's Park	**ITV**
France v Spain	15 June, 6.00 pm, Elland Road	**ITV**
France v Bulgaria	18 June, 4.30 pm, St James's Park	**BBC**
Romania v Spain	18 June, 4.30 pm, Elland Road	**BBC**

Spain

Strip:
Red shirts, dark blue shorts, dark blue socks
Change:
All dark blue with red and yellow trim

Coach:
Javier Clemente

FIFA world ranking:
4

Despite consistently reaching the deciding stages of both the World Cup and European Championship over the past twenty years, Spain's subsequent performances in the finals themselves have never come up to the level expected of them and they have frequently been labelled under-achievers.

In fairness, apart from the dreadful failure in 1982 when, as hosts, they managed only one victory, Spain have played well in the World Cup, and had it not been for Baggio's late goal for Italy two years ago, they might well have reached the semi-finals. But the Spanish press and public expect greater things from their national team, and having experienced huge success, even thirty years ago, it is difficult for them to accept anything less. After Real Madrid's European Cup triumphs in the 1950s, the 1960s proved to be Spain's golden era at both club and international level. The national team won the 1964 European Championship and Barcelona, Real Madrid, Real Zaragoza and Valencia all achieved success in European club competitions.

There are now signs that Spain may be on the threshold of better things once more. The Under-23s won gold at the Barcelona Olympics in 1992 and Spain were unlucky to lose to Italy in their World Cup quarter-final two years later. They dominated the second half of that game, and had Salinas not missed a golden opportunity when clean through on goal the result could have been very different. As it was, Spain lost a game they deserved to win.

Since then, they have continued to improve, and although they failed to qualify for the 1992 European Championship they made no mistake this time round, becoming one of only two countries to qualify with a fixture to spare – and this from a difficult group which contained Denmark, Belgium and the unknown quantity Macedonia.

Spain started their qualifying campaign in fine style with four straight wins, including decisive victories over nearest rivals Denmark (3-0 in Seville) and Belgium (4-1 in Brussels). They lost their 100 per cent record when Belgium held them to a 1-1 draw in Seville, but got back into their stride with a 2-0 win over Armenia. Three more victories and a 1-1 draw at home to Denmark meant that Spain had only dropped four points and, along with France and Russia, had achieved qualification without losing a game.

One would think that a coach who could boast this sort of record would be considered something of a hero but Javier Clemente, who has been in charge of the national side since 1992, has been criticized over his team selection and style of play. He has built a side which has added defensive solidity to Spain's more traditional strengths in midfield and attack, but his detractors claim that he has sacrificed flair to competitiveness and hard work. Yet, although it may not be the most attractive football on display no one can argue that it has not been effective. The veteran goalkeeper Andoni Zubizaretta has been ever-present, keeping six clean sheets and conceding just four goals during qualification. He has been well protected by Rafael Alkorta and Fernandez Abelardo in central defence, while left back Alberto Belsue is a tenacious tackler who can also whip over a mean cross.

José Luís Caminero has formed a good partnership with Julen Guerrero, and the pair are the creative linchpins in midfield. Caminero, a somewhat late arrival to the national team, played particularly well in the 1994 World Cup and his awareness, his threatening runs from central midfield and his ability to take on players has given Spain an extra scoring dimension. Guerrero has blossomed into a fine midfield playmaker. The twenty-two-year-old from Atletico Bilbao was named Spanish Player of the Year last season and alternates between midfield and front-line roles, where his pace, mobility, heading ability, vision and finishing make him a tremendous all-rounder.

Real Madrid's Fernando Hierro is the captain and driving force through the centre of midfield. He is also a devastating finisher and was Spain's top scorer in the qualifiers. His Real Madrid team-mate, Luís Enrique (he of the hide-your-head-in-your-shirt style of goal celebration), is another attack-minded midfielder who covers plenty of ground. During the World Cup finals his ability to keep on running at defenders in the overwhelming heat was a measure of his fitness and raw energy. He ran the Swiss ragged in the second round and celebrated scoring his first international goal in the distinctive style to which we have become accustomed. Enrique was also involved in an incident which might have cost Spain their place in the semi-finals. As the Spanish trailed by 2-1 he moved to meet a cross in the Italian area but met Tassotti's elbow instead.. It should have been a penalty, but the referee missed it, waved play on and Enrique left the pitch for treatment to his injured face. It was a sad end to the tournament for the young player, but he has continued to make impressive progress in the qualifiers for Euro '96.

Caminero, Hierro and Miguel Nadal – an enormous influence as a utility player in the heart of the defence – are admirable for their tireless box-to-box work. All three can operate in defensive roles, but Caminero and Hierro are likely to burst through into scoring positions. The only real weakness appears to be in attack, where Clemente desperately needs to find a replacement for Julio Salinas in the target-man role so crucial for holding up the ball and dragging defenders away to create gaps into which the willing midfielders can run.

Spanish football is awash with talented young players and two in particular are attracting rave reviews. Real Madrid have reportedly already been offered £6 million by Roma for their nineteen-year-old goalscoring sensation Raul Gonzalez. The sublimely talented forward became Real Madrid's youngest-ever debutant at the age of seventeen, scored a hat-trick against Ferencvaros in the Champions League, in which he was second top scorer, and fired home the winner against rivals Barcelona. Not surprisingly, he was voted Most Promising Youngster.

Not to be outdone, Barcelona have their own candidate for future best player in Europe, the shaven-headed Ivan de la Pena. Such has been the hype surrounding the young midfielder that even Cruyff had to somewhat reluctantly respond to calls for him to be given a chance in the first team. Cruyff put him on as a sub against Valladolid, and the twenty-year-old promptly sealed the match by skipping past two defenders and the goalkeeper to tap the ball into the net for a 2-0 victory.

Although it is unlikely that either player will appear in these finals, they are certainly a bit special and could feature in the Olympics Games football competition, where they will aim to retain the title won by the likes of Amavisca, Luís Enrique, Abelardo, Manjarin and Kiko four years ago in Barcelona.

Spain have proved themselves a tricky team to play against, solid at the back with a competitive, hard-working midfield. The main worry for Clemente must be the lack of time he has to prepare the team for the finals: Spain's marathon league doesn't end until thirteen days before the tournament starts.

HOW THEY QUALIFIED

GROUP TWO	P	W	D	L	F	A	PTS
Spain	10	8	2	0	25	4	26
Denmark	10	6	3	1	19	9	21
Belgium	10	4	3	3	17	12	15
Macedonia	10	1	4	5	9	18	7
Cyprus	10	1	4	5	6	20	7
Armenia	10	1	2	7	5	17	5

Cyprus 1 **Spain 2**; Macedonia 1 Denmark 1; Belgium 2 Armenia 0; Armenia 0 Cyprus 0; Denmark 3 Belgium 1; Macedonia 0 **Spain 2**; Belgium 1 Macedonia 1; **Spain 3** Denmark 0; Cyprus 2 Armenia 0; Belgium 1 **Spain 4**; Macedonia 3 Cyprus 0; **Spain 1** Belgium 1; Cyprus 1 Denmark 1; Armenia 0 **Spain 2**; Belgium 2 Cyprus 0; Denmark 1 Macedonia 0; Armenia 2 Macedonia 2; Denmark 4 Cyprus 0; Macedonia 0 Belgium 5; **Spain 1** Armenia 0; Armenia 0 Denmark 2; Belgium 1 Denmark 3; **Spain 6** Cyprus 0; Macedonia 1 Armenia 2; Armenia 0 Belgium 2; Denmark 1 **Spain 1**; Cyprus 1 Macedonia 1; **Spain 3** Macedonia 0; Denmark 3 Armenia 1; Cyprus 1 Belgium 1

PAST PERFORMANCE IN EUROPEAN CHAMPIONSHIP FINALS

Best performance: Winners 1964

Spain entered the inaugural European Championship but withdrew as General Franco did not approve of their quarter-final opponents, the Soviet Union, who had supported the socialists in the Spanish Civil War. With the team they could have fielded, Spain might well have won the competition as Real Madrid were at their absolute peak then. Another opportunity presented itself four years later and this time it was taken. On home ground, Spain beat the Soviet Union 2-1 in the final.

Spain's only other notable performance came in 1984, when they lost to a Platini-inspired French side in the final having looked the more dangerous team for much of the game. They had got there by deservedly beating the reigning champions, West Germany, 1-0 in the group stages and overcoming the talented Danes on penalties in the semi-final.

1960: Quarter-finalists
>First round: Poland 2 Spain 4; Spain 3 Poland 0.
>Quarter-finals: withdrew.

1964: Winners
>First round: Spain 6 Romania 0; Romania 3 Spain 1.
>Second round: Spain 1 Northern Ireland 1;
>Northern Ireland 0 Spain 1.
>Quarter-finals: Spain 5 Republic of Ireland 1;
>Republic of Ireland 0 Spain 2.
>Semi-finals: Spain 2 Hungary 1.
>Final: Spain 2 Soviet Union 1.

1968: Quarter-finalists
>England 1 Spain 0; Spain 1 England 2.

1972: Eliminated in qualifying tournament

1976: Quarter-finalists
>Spain 1 West Germany 1;
>West Germany 2 Spain 0.

1980: First round
Group Two: Italy 0 Spain 0; Spain 1 Belgium 2;
England 2 Spain 1.

1984: Runners-up
Group Two: Spain 1 Romania 1; Portugal 1 Spain 1;
Spain 1 West Germany 0.
Semi-finals: Spain 1 Denmark 1 (5 - 4 pens).
Final: France 2 Spain 0.

1988: First round
Group One: Spain 3 Denmark 2; Italy 1 Spain 0;
West Germany 2 Spain 0.

1992: Eliminated in qualifying tournament

Bulgaria

Strip:
White shirts, green shorts, white socks
Change:
Red shirts, green shorts, red socks

Coach:
Dimitar Penev

FIFA world ranking:
18

In the run-up to the 1994 World Cup the most frequently quoted fact about Bulgaria was their disastrous World Cup record: played 16, won 0. For those struggling to find anything more worthy to mention, there was always the amusing remark that every player's surname ended with a 'v'.

Bulgaria had qualified for the World Cup finals at the expense of a good French team – albeit courtesy of a truly spectacular collapse by France – but that must have seemed a distant memory when they were beaten in their opening game 3-0 by a powerful Nigerian side. Yet with Hristo Stoichkov, Yordan Lechkov and Krasimir Balakov, Bulgaria possessed enough talent to make real progress in the competition, and did not have to be content with merely chalking up a first-ever win. And so it proved.

Subsequent victories over Greece and a Maradona-less Argentina saw them through to face Mexico in the second round, where Stoichkov, who in the early games could have taught Grumpy a few lessons, displayed his trademark speed, strength and powerful finishing to put Bulgaria into the lead. The referee was handing out yellow cards like party invitations and Mexico's equalizer was something of a gift – a dubious penalty that even the Mexican players seemed surprised at being awarded. With no further goals the game went to penalties and, as if to make amends, Mexico missed theirs with some style and the Bulgarian adventure continued.

The quarter-final against Germany was one of <u>the</u> most exciting games in World Cup history. Germany took the lead with a second-half penalty but Stoichkov curled a brilliant free kick over the wall and beyond a statue-like Illgner. Three minutes later, as the buzz was still dying down, Lechkov's header put Bulgaria into the semi-finals. The unbelievable had happened.

In the semis, Bulgaria were unlucky to meet an Italian side which, having scraped through thus far, chose this game to perform in the style which had been so eagerly anticipated. In a dazzling first-half spell, Roberto Baggio scored two corkers and although Stoichkov pulled one back from yet another penalty, Italy hung on.

Bulgaria had gone further than they could have believed possible in their wildest dreams. Yet, given a little more fortune with refereeing decisions, they might even have reached the final. As it was, their efforts had left them mentally and physically drained and they failed to lift themselves for the third-place play-off against Sweden.

Once all the excitement had died down, the question was: were Bulgaria a flash in the pan, or had they finally broken into Europe's elite? Could they repeat their World Cup success and qualify for the European Championship finals for the first time? It didn't take long to find out. Drawn in what was a tough-looking qualifying group with Germany, Moldova, Georgia and Wales, Bulgaria won their first four games with ease. Then in June came the eagerly awaited home tie against Germany – the first meeting between the two teams since that memorable World Cup quarter-final. Germany took a seemingly unassailable 2-0 lead but Bulgaria got back into the game with two goals from Stoichkov before Emil Kostadinov grabbed a last-gasp winner to confirm Bulgaria as Germany's *bête noir*.

Virtually assured of qualification, Bulgaria surrendered their 100 per cent record with an away draw in Albania and despite winning the return tie they were then surprisingly beaten away to Georgia – a result which left them level on points with Germany, their opponents in their final game. A capacity crowd in Berlin's Olympic Stadium watched in disbelief as Stoichkov scored his tenth goal of the qualifiers early in the second half, but Klinsmann equalized within three minutes and Hassler's excellent free kick put the German's ahead. There was to be no glorious recovery this time, and Klinsmann secured the game by converting a seventy-sixth-minute penalty to put his team at the top of the group.

With no outstanding replacements for the class of '94, many

familiar names will again be on show in England, providing dash and enterprise up front, skill and creativity in midfield and the occasional slip-up in defence. Stoichkov appears to have settled in at Parma, after a long and bitter dispute with Johan Cruyff forced him to leave Barcelona, where he had enjoyed so much success. The Barca fans may never forgive Cruyff for losing the fiery but supremely talented Bulgarian. The thirty-year-old striker may not be as quick as he was, but he remains one of only a handful of players in the world who can single-handedly change a game.

His striking partner, Kostadinov, is currently kicking his heels on the Bayern Munich subs bench alongside France's Jean-Pierre Papin, and when he has been used it has been in midfield rather than in his favoured attacking role. Obviously, this is the risk players take when they sign for a big club saturated with internationals.

Contrary to popular myth, the hirsutely challenged Lechkov hasn't hung up his boots in favour of a free bus pass. The scorer of Bulgaria's World Cup-winner against Germany is in fact only twenty-eight years old and along with England's Steve Stone and Spain's Luís Enrique will be promoting the close-shorn hairstyle in the finals. Lechkov is the creative heart of the team and dictates play for Bulgaria in midfield. He has great vision, tactical awareness and can make devastating attacking runs into the area. He picked up an injury during the game against Germany in November and was out of Bundesliga action for several weeks, but he should recover in plenty of time.

Although Stoichkov may be the star, the mainstay of the team is thirty-year-old Krasimir Balakov, who also plays his club football in Germany. Balakov played every minute of Bulgaria's historic World Cup campaign and was an ever-present during their qualification games. He puts in an enormous amount of work all over midfield and is always available to help out the more stately Lechkov. He gives Bulgaria options in attack and at set pieces. His contribution was recognized by his inclusion in the official World Cup Select team chosen by FIFA.

Borislav Mikhailov, the most famous possessor of a toupee after Burt Reynolds, is still at his eccentric best in goal despite playing for Reading, and the committed defender Ivanov will no doubt still be prepared to throw his body in front of anything to protect the goal, even if it necessitates hospital treatment.

One important boost during the qualifying matches has been the return of the coach's nephew, Luboslav Penev, whose battle with testicular cancer forced him to miss Bulgaria's World Cup campaign. His speed and movement off the ball creating space for Kostadinov and Stoichkov to exploit have been highly praised. Penev is a key player for Atlético Madrid, for whom he has scored crucial goals, including two in their 3-1 defeat of Barcelona.

The bulk of the team play outside Bulgaria and the result is a poor domestic game – not one club side reached the second round in European competitions – but a flourishing national side. No one will treat Bulgaria lightly this time round.

HOW THEY QUALIFIED

GROUP SEVEN	P	W	D	L	F	A	PTS
Germany	10	8	1	1	27	10	25
Bulgaria	10	7	1	2	24	10	22
Georgia	10	5	0	5	14	13	15
Moldova	10	3	0	7	11	27	9
Wales	10	2	2	6	9	19	8
Albania	10	2	2	6	10	16	8

Wales 2 Albania 0; Georgia 0 Moldova 1; Moldova 3 Wales 2; **Bulgaria 2** Georgia 0; Albania 1 Germany 2; Georgia 5 Wales 0; **Bulgaria 4** Moldova 1; Albania 0 Georgia 1; Wales 0 **Bulgaria 3**; Moldova 0 Germany 3; Germany 2 Albania 1; Georgia 0 Germany 2; **Bulgaria 3** Wales 1; Albania 3 Moldova 0; Germany 1 Wales 1; Moldova 0 **Bulgaria 3**; Georgia 2 Albania 0; **Bulgaria 3** Germany 2; Wales 0 Georgia 1; Moldova 2 Albania 3; Germany 4 Georgia 1; Wales 1 Moldova 0; Albania 1 **Bulgaria 1**; **Bulgaria 3** Albania 0; Germany 6 Moldova 1; Wales 1 Germany 2; Georgia 2 **Bulgaria 1**; Germany 3 **Bulgaria 1**; Albania 1 Wales 1; Moldova 3 Georgia 2

PAST PERFORMANCE IN EUROPEAN CHAMPIONSHIP FINALS

Best performance: Quarter-finalists 1968

Bulgaria's best showing in the European Championship was in 1968 when they were, the current team apart, probably at their peak. The inspirational Georgi Asparoukhov, whom many people rate as the best player ever from Bulgaria, led the attack, joined by Hristo Bonev and Petar Jokev. Bulgaria qualified ahead of the much-fancied Portuguese, who had thrilled everyone in the World Cup two years previously, and met Italy in the quarter-finals. They won their home leg in Sofia 3-2 but faced an intimidating crowd in Naples and lost 2-0.

Since then Bulgaria have failed to reach the finals of the European Championship and have seldom even come close. Their best effort was in 1988, when they finished runners-up to the Republic of Ireland.

1960: **First round**
Yugoslavia 2 Bulgaria 0; Bulgaria 1 Yugoslavia 1.
1964: **Second round**
First round: Bulgaria 3 Portugal 1; Portugal 3 Bulgaria 1; Bulgaria 1 Portugal 0 (Rome).
Second round: Bulgaria 1 France 0; France 3 Bulgaria 1.
1968: **Quarter-finalists**
Bulgaria 3 Italy 2; Italy 2 Bulgaria 0.
1972-92: **Eliminated in qualifying round**

Romania

Strip:
All yellow with red and blue trim
Change:
All red with yellow and blue trim

Coach:
Anghel Iordanescu

FIFA world ranking:
11

After years in the wilderness, Romania blossomed into one of the sensations of the 1994 World Cup finals. Against Colombia, one of the pre-tournament favourites, they produced the first upset of the finals with a 3-1 victory, achieved through their classic counter-attacking style. Colombia dominated the play and possession but were never able to breach the Romanian defence and two goals by Florin Raducioiu and one from Gheorghe Hagi – an amazing dipping cross-shot from fully 35 yards – sealed an impressive start.

In their next game, Romania's tactics of defending with a six-man midfield were exposed by the Swiss, who beat them easily, but victory over the hosts earned Romania a second-round tie against Argentina. Once again, Argentina were afforded plenty of time and space to stroke the ball around but were constantly caught on the break. Ilie Dumitrescu opened the scoring for Romania with a curling free kick which deceived Islas in the Argentian goal as effectively as Hagi had mesmerised Colombia's goalkeeper, Cordoba.

The second Romanian goal was typically clinical in its speed and execution. Dumitrescu cut through the middle and fed Hagi on the right. His defence-splitting pass was coolly tucked inside the near post by Dumitrescu. The roles of scorer and provider were reversed when Romania went three up: Tibor Selymes broke down the left, squared the ball to Dumitrescu who flicked it into Hagi's path for him to score with a glorious, rising drive. The Argentinian defence were left labouring behind like naive schoolboys.

Romania lost on penalties to Sweden in the quarter-final and missed out on what would have been a potentially fascinating encounter with Brazil, but they had proved they were among the very best in the competition. Coach Anghel Iordanescu has remained faithful to his World Cup stars and the team that qualified for the European Championship was practically unchanged from the one that lost to Sweden – nine men from that game played in Romania's final European Championship qualifier, a 2-0 victory over Slovakia in November. This continuity means that Iordanescu's squad of experienced internationals are totally confident and at home with the team's tactics and style of play.

Romania's performances during qualification were steady rather than spectacular, although they were always favourites to win their group. A surprising home defeat against France was the only real wobble, and in the main they did just enough to qualify.

The forward line of Hagi, Dumitrescu and Raducioiu has been enhanced by the return of thirty-two-year-old Marius Lacatus, who is back playing his club football with Steaua Bucharest after spells in Spain and Italy. He was a star of the 1990 World Cup team and has an excellent understanding with Hagi. Although probably not the first choice, he is a valuable player to have in the squad and proved as much with three goals during qualification.

A lot has been said and written about Hagi, who is undoubtedly one of the world's best players. He has exceptional skill and often takes up a deep position from which it is difficult for opposing players to pick him up. He is at his most dangerous when running at defences or launching swift counter-attacks in tandem with the likes of Lacatus, Raducioiu and Dumitrescu.

At present, Hagi is more often than not kicking his heels on the Barcelona subs' bench, but lack of first-team football should not be a problem for him. He was outstanding against Slovakia and seems better suited to the format of a major tournament, where he can release his full creative flow.

Romania's main strength is that they are a precise passing team in every position. In defence, Gica Popescu and Dan Petrescu are as adept at starting an attack as stopping one, and the same goes for the versatile defender Daniel Prodan, who plays either in midfield or as a sweeper for Steaua Bucharest. Tibor Selymes, Dorinel Munteanu and Ioan Lupescu are all experienced internationals and have built up a good interaction through playing alongside one another for such a long time. As a result, Romania are capable of launching counter-attacks from any part of the pitch and, as Colombia and Argentina discovered to their cost, it's not how much possession you have, it's what you do with it.

HOW THEY QUALIFIED

GROUP ONE	P	W	D	L	F	A	PTS
Romania	10	6	3	1	18	9	21
France	10	5	5	0	22	2	20
Slovakia	10	4	2	4	14	18	14
Poland	10	3	4	3	14	12	13
Israel	10	3	3	4	13	13	12
Azerbaijan	10	0	1	9	2	29	1

Israel 2 Poland 1; Slovakia 0 France 0; **Romania 3** Azerbaijan 0; France 0 **Romania 0**; Israel 2 Slovakia 2; Poland 1 Azerbaijan 0; **Romania 3** Slovakia 2; Poland 0 France 0; Azerbaijan 0 Israel 2; Azerbaijan 0 France 2; Israel 1 **Romania 1**; **Romania 2** Poland 1; Israel 0 France 0; Slovakia 4 Azerbaijan 1; Poland 4 Israel 3; France 4 Slovakia 0; Azerbaijan 1 **Romania 4**; Poland 5 Slovakia 0; **Romania 2** Israel 1; France 1 Poland 1; Azerbiajan 0 Slovakia 1; France 10 Azerbaijan 0; Slovkia 1 Israel 0; Poland 0 **Romania 0**; **Romania 1** France 3; Israel 2 Azerbiajan 0; Slovakia 4 Poland 1; Slovakia 0 **Romania 2**; Azerbiajan 0 Poland 0; France 2 Israel 0

PAST PERFORMANCE IN EUROPEAN CHAMPIONSHIP FINALS

Best performance: Quarter-finalists 1960, 1972

Until the 1980s, Romania had never really featured in either World Cup or European Championship finals other than their quarter-final appearances in 1972. In the eighties, Steaua Bucharest (the army team) and Dinamo Bucharest (the police team), the two clubs which had dominated Romanian football in the post-war period, became, under the direct influence of the ruling regime, even stronger.

In Romania they were almost unbeatable, totally dominating

domestic football, and in 1986 Steaua became the first Eastern European side to win the European Cup. As they formed the core of the national team, this marked the start of Romania's most successful period, although their improvement has yet to be significantly rewarded in the European Championship. With the downfall of the Ceaucescu regime players such as Hagi, Popescu and Lacatus have been in great demand from foreign clubs, particularly after their 1990 World Cup performance.

1960:   **Quarter-finalists**
First round: Romania 3 Turkey 0; Turkey 2 Romania 0.
Quarter-final: Romania 0 Czechoslovakia 2.

1964:   **First round**
Spain 6 Romania 0; Romania 3 Spain 1.

1968:   **Eliminated in qualifying tournament**

1972:   **Quarter-finalists**
Hungary 1 Romania 1; Romania 2 Hungary 2;
Hungary 2 Romania 1 (Belgrade).

1976-80: **Eliminated in qualifying tournament**

1984:   **First round**
Group Two: Spain 1 Romania 1;
West Germany 2 Romania 1; Portugal 1 Romania 0

1988-92: **Eliminated in qualifying tournament**

France

Strip:
Blue shirt, white shorts, red socks
Change:
White shirts, blue shorts, red socks

Coach:
Aimé Jacquet

FIFA world ranking:
13

France were one of the teams expected to challenge for the 1994 World Cup but they didn't even make it to the finals. They needed only one point from their last two home games, against Israel and Bulgaria, but they contrived to lose them both, succumbing to injury-time winners on each occasion. Not surprisingly, perhaps, French coach Gerard Houllier was replaced by his assistant, Aimé Jacquet, in December 1993. Under Jacquet's guidance France have remained unbeaten and conceded just two goals during their qualification for the European Championship finals.

France started their campaign as if still dazed by their World Cup disaster. Four goalless draws in their first five games and an uninspiring 2-0 win over Azerbaijan left them in third place behind Romania and Israel, and public discontent about the national team's inability to score was understandable.

Temporary relief was provided with a 4-0 win against Slovakia, but the French again flirted with danger in a 1-1 draw at home to Poland (a result saved by Paris Saint-Germain's impressive striker Youri Djorkaeff, who scored from a free kick six minutes from time). Although this was the first goal the solid defence had conceded, public impatience was rising and Jacquet was forced by injuries and suspensions, to introduce new players, such as Bordeaux's promising striker Zinedine Zidane, for the next game, against Azerbaijan. The tactic worked as France romped to their biggest win, with eight players, including debutant Zidane, scoring in the 10-0 victory.

The French travelled to Bucharest with renewed confidence the following month and put in their best performance to emerge emphatic 3-1 winners. The bold Jacquet had changed his team around, nervelessly leaving out both Eric Cantona and David Ginola and deploying Marcel Desailly's powerful presence in the back four rather than in his customary midfield role. Romania hadn't lost at home for five years but France took the game by the scruff of the neck from the start. Christian Karembeu displayed the power, versatility and drive in midfield that had persuaded Sampdoria to offer French champions Nantes £3 million for his services. He has become a big favourite with the fans in Genoa and crowned a brilliant performance against Romania by scoring the all-important first goal. Further efforts from Djorkaeff and Zidane sealed a fine victory.

France completed their qualifying programme with an unconvincing 2-0 win over Israel, but the result at least ensured qualification, and they squeezed past Holland and the Republic of Ireland as the sixth-best second-placed team.

Jacquet has a wealth of talent to take to England and he has been prepared to sacrifice individuals in his quest for a harmonious, smooth-running team: neither Ginola, Cantona nor Jean-Pierre Papin figured in the final qualifying games. At the back, goalkeeper Bernard Lama kept eight clean sheets in the early-stage matches, which was in no little way thanks to the tight defence organized around Jocelyn Angloma, Laurent Blanc, Alain Roche and Eric di Meco.

There are also plenty of lively performers up front. Karembeu has been the driving force in midfield. He's athletic, never stops running and makes things happen, but if he's not on song, as in the game against Israel, the whole midfield suffers. Djorkaeff ended the qualifying stages as France's top scorer with five goals in four consecutive games, and distinguished himself as an all-round attacking midfielder. His free kick saved the day against Poland and probably did as much as anything to confirm his place in the team. His Paris Saint-Germain team-mate, striker Patrice Loko, is talented if somewhat erratic, while Zidane has also shown considerable promise.

In addition, the French have one consistent and truly world-class player in the imposing figure of Marcel Desailly. The Ghanian-born defender or midfielder possesses skill, vision and above all power, and it is his great strength which makes him such an effective player. For Milan, he operates in front of the back four, linking with Zvonimir

Boban and Demetrio Albertini, occasionally pushing further forward with surging runs. Desailly is also a pillar of impregnability in defence, almost impossible to beat man to man in terms of either strength or speed. It was in the centre of Marseille's defence that Desailly came to wider attention in the 1993 European Cup final, when he virtually shut Milan's great striker Marco van Basten out of the game. Two weeks after their triumph, Marseille were plunged into a match-fixing scandal and were forced to sell players. Milan snapped up Desailly, and one year later he was their best player in the 4-0 demolition of Barcelona, which earned him the distinction of being the only player to have won the European Cup in successive seasons with different clubs. He has moved back into central defence for France, but such is his versatility that he is a prize asset and will surely be one of the best players in the tournament.

Yet Jacquet still lacks a charismatic leader in attack, and although he obviously doesn't hold Cantona and Ginola in quite the same reverence as they do at Old Trafford and St James' Park, both players could provide the necessary technique and flair. Cantona, in particular, can provide subtlety and vision to link defence and attack, which he does so brilliantly for Manchester United. He can hold the ball up and wait for support, lay it off with a simple ball, or spread the play across the field. His range of talents should find a home in the French side, but his inclusion would change what is now a successful formation and force Jacquet into rethinking his tactics.

The presence of Zidane and Loko suggest that Papin may have to wait some time to regain his place. The thirty-two-year-old striker has struggled to claim a regular berth for his club, Bayern Munich, following an operation on his knee two seasons ago, and participated in only a handful of the qualifying games. He is a valuable player to have on call, though.

While France were one of only three teams to qualify unbeaten and are showing signs of finding their form, it is worth remembering that they qualified for the 1992 European Championship with an equally good record under Michel Platini, only to prove a huge disappointment in the finals. The team will also have one eye on what will be considered the greater prize in two years' time, when France host the World Cup.

HOW THEY QUALIFIED

GROUP ONE	P	W	D	L	F	A	PTS
Romania	10	6	3	1	18	9	21
France	10	5	5	0	22	2	20
Slovakia	10	4	2	4	14	18	14
Poland	10	3	4	3	14	12	13
Israel	10	3	3	4	13	13	12
Azerbaijan	10	0	1	9	2	29	1

Israel 2 Poland 1; Slovakia 0 **France 0**; Romania 3 Azerbaijan 0; **France 0** Romania 0; Israel 2 Slovakia 2; Poland 1 Azerbaijan 0; Romania 3 Slovakia 2; Poland 0 **France 0**; Azerbaijan 0 Israel 2; Azerbaijan 0 **France 2**; Israel 1 Romania 1; Romania 2 Poland 1; Israel 0 **France 0**; Slovakia 4 Azerbaijan 1; Poland 4 Israel 3; **France 4** Slovakia 0; Azerbaijan 1 Romania 4; Poland 5 Slovakia 0; Romania 2 Israel 1; **France 1** Poland 1; Azerbiajan 0 Slovakia 1; **France 10** Azerbaijan 0; Slovkia 1 Israel 0; Poland 0 Romania 0; Romania 1 **France 3**; Israel 2 Azerbiajan 0; Slovakia 4 Poland 1; Slovakia 0 Romania 2; Azerbiajan 0 Poland 0; **France 2** Israel 0.

PAST PERFORMANCE IN EUROPEAN CHAMPIONSHIP FINALS

Best performance: Winners 1984

Semi-final losers (5-4 to Yugoslavia) in 1960, France reached the last eight in the next two championships before going into a disastrous slump. They failed to reach the finals again until 1984 when, inspired by the artistry and goals of Michel Platini, they became champions for the first time, beating Spain 2-0 in the final. That great team quickly disintegrated and France failed to qualify for the 1988 finals. Platini worked his magic again, this time as manager, to make them the most impressive qualifiers in 1992, but their showing in the finals was very disappointing.

1960:   **Fourth**
First round: France 7 Greece 1; Greece 1 France 1.
Quarter-final: France 5 Austria 2; Austria 2 France 4.
Semi-final: Yugoslavia 5 France 4.
Third-place play-off: Czechoslovakia 2 France 0.

1964:   **Quarter-finalists**
First round: England 1 France 1; France 5 England 2.
Second round: Bulgaria 1 France 0; France 3 Bulgaria 1.
Quarter-final: France 1 Hungary 3.

1968:   **Quarter-finalists**
Quarter-final: France 1 Yugoslavia 1;
Yugoslavia 5 France 1.

1972-80:   **Eliminated in qualifying tournament**

1984:   **Winners**
Group One: France 1 Denmark 0; France 5 Belgium 0;
France 3 Yugoslavia 2.
Semi-final: France 3 Portugal 2 (aet).
Final: France 2 Spain 0.

1988:   **Eliminated in qualifying tournament**

1992:   **First round**
Group One: Sweden 1 France 1; France 0 England 0;
Denmark 2 France 1.

Group C

Germany, Czech Republic, Italy, Russia

Each major championship has its so-called 'group of death' and Group C is it. For a start, of the four teams, only Italy failed to win their qualifying group but the challenge goes deeper than that. All four countries have, in one form or other, won the European Championship: as West Germany, Czechoslovakia, the Soviet Union and, er, Italy. For that reason alone, this is going to be one of the most absorbing arenas of the finals.

Germany are the seeded team and marginal group favourites. They are the only side to have won the tournament twice, and despite their earlier-than-expected exit from the 1994 World Cup finals, they qualified impressively enough. However, that defeat by Bulgaria proved that Germany are beatable and the aura of invincibility that used to surround the German national team has been ripped apart. Because of their reputation they had, in effect, a one-goal advantage before the game had even started but that defeat will now have every other team thinking, 'If Bulgaria can do it, so can we.'

Having said that, the Czech Republic do not look strong enough to beat Germany in the opening game and thus to repeat their historic victory in the 1976 final. They were too inconsistent in the qualifying tournament, and although they performed better against quality opposition, their sequence of matches – Germany, Italy then Russia – is probably the worst possible.

The battle for the two qualifying positions will probably be between the remaining three teams, and the games on 11, 16 and 19

June will be crucial. This is going to be dreadfully close. The Russians are a difficult team to assess. Although they were drawn in one of the easier qualifying groups, there can be no question about the ease with which they reached these finals. Italy are brimming with talent and should qualify but they are notoriously slow starters and defeat by Russia at Anfield could ruin their chances before they've really got going. However, no matter how desperate things become for Italy, they possess individuals who can convert a lost cause into victory, no matter how impossible that seems. Roberto Baggio did it for them in the last World Cup and either he, Del Pierro or Zola could do it again.

That leaves Russia against Germany as the crunch game, on 16 June. Germany have the better record between the two, but with Andrei Kanchelskis renewing his acquaintance with the Old Trafford pitch on which he terrorized defences for Manchester United, it could be a very tight thing indeed.

Germany v Czech Republic	9 June 5.00 pm, Old Trafford	**BBC**
Italy v Russia	11 June, 4.30 pm, Anfield	**BBC**
Czech Republic v Italy	14 June, 7.30 pm, Anfield	**ITV**
Russia v Germany	16 June, 3.00 pm, Old Trafford	**ITV**
Russia v Czech Republic	19 June, 7.30 pm, Anfield	**BBC**
Italy v Germany	19 June, 7.30 pm, Old Trafford	**BBC**

Germany

Strip:
White shirts, black shorts white socks
Change:
Green shirts, white shorts, green socks

Coach:
Berti Vogts

FIFA world ranking:
2

During Germany's quarter-final match against Bulgaria in the 1994 World Cup, German defender Martin Wagner was knocked unconcious and substituted shortly after Lothar Matthäus had put his team into the lead. When Wagner came round he asked: 'Is it still 1-0?' Told by a coach that it had finished 2-1, Wagner asked: 'Who scored our second?'

That it might have been Bulgaria who were through to the semi-finals – as indeed it was, courtesy of Stoichkov and Lechkov – was obviously not a possibility he had even remotely considered. Wagner's assumption highlights the fundamental quality which has brought Germany such phenomenal success. The players have a positive, winning attitude which, coupled with an amazing resilience, has made them the most successful team in the European Championship. In their last six appearances they have reached the final four times, winning the competition twice. And for good measure, in the intervening years, they have won the World Cup twice and finished runners-up twice. You can never discount Germany, no matter what the score, no matter how little time is left to play. They've made more comebacks than Gary Glitter.

Perhaps because of this, Bulgaria's victory in the World Cup was gleefully received worldwide, except, of course in Germany. The national side, the unified country's pride and joy, had been beaten at an inconceivably premature stage, and when their Euro '96 qualification hit a sticky patch with a home draw against Wales and a 3-2 defeat by Bulgaria after four consecutive victories, stinging criticism of the team and manager Berti Vogts was heard on an almost unprecedented scale.

Vogts was in an unenviable position. His four predecessors, Sepp Herberger (1936-63), Helmut Schoen (1964-78), Jupp Derwall (1984-90), and Franz Beckenbauer (1984-90), had all won either the World Cup or European Championship or both. Vogts' team had finished runners-up in the 1992 European Championship but now his leadership was blamed and he was accused of picking new talent only when his veterans were unavailable.

The backlash came just as the Bundesliga was growing massively in popularity, thanks to the return of players such as Jürgen Klinsmann, Lothar Matthäus, Andy Moller and Jurgen Kohler from foreign clubs and, probably for the first time ever, the German league was attracting more support from television and fans than the national side.

Maybe it was all a ruse to lure the rest of the world into a false sense of security by suggesting that Germany was an ailing force. After all, the team had been criticized before and had nearly always come good. German fears that their side might finish only second in the group were premature: in their next game, against Georgia, they won 4-1; against Moldova they cruised home 6-1, and three days later they beat Wales 2-1. Germany were now on equal points with Bulgaria, and despite going 1-0 down to an early goal from Stoichkov, they gained a small measure of revenge with a 3-1 victory. German skipper Klinsmann scored two of the goals to take his international tally to thirty-four. His excellent scoring form for Bayern Munich and his country will be a vital factor if Germany are to go one better this year. However, he also collected a second booking in the win over Bulgaria and will therefore miss the first game in England.

Vogts has tended to draw his squad mainly from Bayern Munich and Borussia Dortmund. In fact the great German team of 1972 used a similar tactic, the presence of six Bayern men and three from Borussia Moenchengladbach creating a greater understanding between the players. But whether this present team can repeat those successes is another matter. Not every player has been producing the consistent form required for the finals, where they will play three games in one week.

Of the newcomers, Heiko Herrlich has formed a good partnership with Klinsmann. The tall centre forward, who was joint top scorer in the Bundesliga last year, moved from Borussia Moenchengladbach to Borussia Dortmund for a German domestic record of £4.5 million last summer and scored his first international goal on his second appearance, against Wales.

Herrlich shared the top-scoring honours with Mario Basler, one of the most spectacular performers in the Bundesliga last season. Super Mario is a midfielder, which makes his goalscoring record even more remarkable, and excels in well-timed runs and decisive finishing. The twenty-seven-year-old is also renowned as a dead-ball specialist, equally adept at curling the ball around the wall or simply powering it from long range.

Basler will most likely partner Thomas Hassler and Andy Moller in a strong midfield line-up. Hassler, himself an excellent scorer from free kicks, was the most creative player in the last championship, while Moller can be technically brilliant on his day. Genuinely two-footed, his skill is matched by a wonderful turn of speed.

Although the German defence conceded a surprisingly high number of goals during the qualifying matches they now possess, in the form of Matthias Sammer, the best German *libero* since Beckenbauer. He was the first East German to appear in the united team and is the creative linchpin in defence.

HOW THEY QUALIFIED

GROUP SEVEN	P	W	D	L	F	A	PTS
Germany	10	8	1	1	27	10	25
Bulgaria	10	7	1	2	24	10	22
Georgia	10	5	0	5	14	13	15
Moldova	10	3	0	7	11	27	9
Wales	10	2	2	6	9	19	8
Albania	10	2	2	6	10	16	8

Wales 2 Albania 0; Georgia 0 Moldova 1; Moldova 3 Wales 2;
Bulgaria 2 Georgia 0; Albania 1 **Germany 2**; Georgia 5 Wales 0;
Bulgaria 4 Moldova 1; Albania 0 Georgia 1; Wales 0 Bulgaria 3;
Moldova 0 **Germany 3**; **Germany 2** Albania 1; Georgia 0
Germany 2; Bulgaria 3 Wales 1; Albania 3 Moldova 0;
Germany 1 Wales 1; Moldova 0 Bulgaria 3; Georgia 2 Albania 0;
Bulgaria 3 **Germany 2**; Wales 0 Georgia 1; Moldova 2 Albania 3;
Germany 4 Georgia 1; Wales 1 Moldova 0; Albania 1 Bulgaria 1;
Bulgaria 3 Albania 0; **Germany 6** Moldova 1; Wales 1 **Germany 2**;
Georgia 2 Bulgaria 1; **Germany 3** Bulgaria 1; Albania 1 Wales 1;
Moldova 3 Georgia 2.

PAST PERFORMANCE IN EUROPEAN CHAMPIONSHIP FINALS
(as West Germany before 1992)

Best performance: Winners 1972, 1980

The track records of the two nations that make up the united
German team could not be more different. While East Germany's
best performance was to reach the second round in 1964, West
Germany, who did not compete until 1968, are the only nation to
have won the title twice: in 1972 (3-0 against the Soviet Union) and
1980 (2-1 against Belgium). Between those victories, they lost the
1976 final on penalties to Czechoslovakia.

In 1988, West Germany lost on home territory in the semi-finals
to a last-minute winner from Holland's Van Basten and four years ago
the united side reached yet another final, only to be confounded by

the hard-working Danes, who deservedly won 2-0 with a tremendous counter-attacking style.

1960-64: **Did not enter**
1968: **Eliminated in qualifying tournament**
1972: **Winners**
Quarter-final: England 1 West Germany 3;
West Germany 0 England 0.
Semi-final: West Germany 2 Belgium 1.
Final: West Germany 3 Soviet Union 0.
1976: **Runners-up**
Quarter-final: Spain 1 West Germany 1;
West Germany 2 Spain 0.
Semi-final: West Germany 4 Yugoslavia 2 (aet).
Final: Czechoslovakia 2 West Germany 2 (5-3 pen.).
1980: **Winners**
Group One: West Germany 1 Czechoslvakia 0;
West Germany 3 Holland 2; West Germany 0 Greece 0.
Final: West Germany 2 Belgium 1.
1984: **First round**
Portugal 0 West Germany 0; West Germany 2
Romania 1; Spain 1 West Germany 0.
1988: **Semi-finalists**
Group One: West Germany 1 Italy 1; West Germany 2
Denmark 0; West Germany 2 Spain 0.
Semi-finals: West Germany 1 Holland 2.
1992: **Runners-up**
Group Two: Germany 1 CIS 1; Germany 2 Scotland 0;
Holland 3 Germany 1.
Semi-final: Germany 3 Sweden 2.
Final: Denmark 2 Germany 0.

Czech Republic

Strip:
Red shirts, white shorts, blue socks
Change:
All white

Coach:
Dusan Uhrin

FIFA world ranking:
14

The Czech Republic could not have fancied their chances when they were drawn with Holland and Norway but following good performances against both these teams they finished top of their group. In fact, the only major obstacle to qualification came from lowly Luxembourg, who condemned the Czechs to the most humiliating defeat in their history.

Inconsistency was a feature of the Czechs' qualification. After thrashing Malta 6-1 they could manage only a 0-0 draw with them the following month. Then, after producing a world-class performance in Prague to beat the Dutch 3-1, they turned in a desperate one to lose to Luxembourg as Guy Hellers' last-minute strike gave the Grand Duchy a famous victory.

Despite these shaky results, the Czechs raised their game when they needed to. In November they travelled to Holland and came away with a 0-0 draw, even though they were without their talismanic striker, Tomas Skuhravy, who had fallen out with coach Dusan Uhrin. Skuhravy missed the following game too, a 4-2 victory over Belarus in which the exciting young midfielder Patrik Berger scored twice. The striker was recalled for the home tie against Holland and celebrated a successful reconciliation with Uhrin with a forty-ninth minute equalizer. Further goals from Vaclav Nemecek and Berger in the space of thirteen minutes gave the Czechs a well-deserved win.

Following the aberration against Luxembourg, the Czechs held the runaway leaders Norway to a 1-1 draw away before beating them at home with goals from Skuhravy and Radek Drulak. That still left the Czechs five points behind Norway, but wins in their final two games, away to Belarus and home to Luxembourg, and Norway's defeat in Holland were enough to ensure their qualification.

The Czechs have a tough, well-balanced side with a core of experienced internationals, such as Miroslav Kadlec in defence, Nemecek in midfield and Skuhravy up front. Nor do they rely too heavily on exiles and substantial contributions still come from Sparta and Slavia Prague, who both had good runs in European club competitions.

Perhaps the most exciting prospect for the finals is twenty-two-year-old midfielder Patrik Berger, who plays for Borussia Dortmund. He proved the revelation of the qualifiers, scoring six of his eight international goals in European Championship matches, and is the sort of attacking player who will trouble most defences with late runs into the penalty area.

Skuhravy's centre-forward position, for so long automatically his domain, is under threat from Drulak who, at thirty-four, is one of the oldest players in the team and something of a late developer. In December Skuhravy joined Sporting Lisbon from Genoa in a loan move which he hoped would win him back a permanent place in the national team following speculation that he would miss out on the trip to England.

The nation's joy at reaching their first European Championship finals as a separate republic was tempered by the draw which pitched them in the same group as Russia, Germany and Italy, but the Czechs are probably at their best against quality teams.

HOW THEY QUALIFIED

GROUP FIVE	P	W	D	L	F	A	PTS
Czech Rep	10	6	3	1	21	6	21
Holland	10	6	2	2	23	5	20
Norway	10	6	2	2	17	7	20
Belarus	10	3	2	5	8	13	11
Luxembourg	10	3	1	6	3	21	10
Malta	10	0	2	8	2	22	2

Czech Republic 6 Malta 1; Luxembourg 0 Holland 4; Norway 1 Belarus 0; Malta 0 **Czech Republic 0**; Belarus 2 Luxembourg 0; Norway 1 Holland 1; Belarus 0 Norway 4; Holland 0 **Czech Republic 0**; Malta 0 Norway 1; Holland 5 Luxembourg 0; Malta 0 Luxembourg 0; **Czech Republic 4** Belarus 2; Luxembourg 0 Norway 2; Holland 4 Malta 0; Belarus 1 Malta 1; **Czech Republic 3** Holland 1; Norway 5 Luxembourg 0; Belarus 1 Holland 0; Luxembourg 1 **Czech Republic 0**; Norway 2 Malta 0; Norway 1 **Czech Republic 1**; **Czech Republic 2** Norway 0; Luxembourg 1 Malta 0; Holland 1 Belarus 0; Belarus 0 **Czech Republic 2**; Malta 0 Holland 4; Luxembourg 0 Belarus 0; Malta 0 Belarus 2; **Czech Republic 3** Luxembourg 0; Holland 3 Norway 0.

PAST PERFORMANCE IN EUROPEAN CHAMPIONSHIP FINALS
(as Czechoslovakia)

Best performance: Winners 1976

Czechoslovakia ceased to exist as a footballing nation when the Czech Republic and Slovakia went their separate ways in 1994. In certain golden periods throughout its history as a unified country, Czechoslovakia had been at the forefront of world football. The army team, Dukla Prague, formed the basis of the national side which finished third in the inaugural championship in 1960 and reached the final of the 1962 World Cup. However, Czechoslovakia's biggest success came in 1976, when they finished ahead of England in the qualifying tournament and beat the Soviet Union in the quarter-finals to set up a semi-final against the World Cup runners-up, Holland.

Greater unity and spirit saw Czechoslovakia beat the Dutch super-stars 3-1 and in a thrilling final they deservedly beat world champions Germany, even if the game was decided on penalties.

With many of their influential players still around, Czechoslovakia finished third in the 1980 finals but since then results have been poor and they failed to qualify for the subsequent following three championships.

1960:   **Third place**
Preliminary round:
Republic of Ireland 2 Czechoslovakia 0;
Czechoslovakia 4 Republic of Ireland 0.
First round: Denmark 2 Czechoslovakia 2;
Czechoslovakia 5 Denmark 1.
Quarter-final: Romania 0 Czechoslovakia 2;
Czechoslovakia 3 Romania 0.
Semi-final: Soviet Union 3 Czechoslovakia 0.
Third-place play-off: Czechoslovakia 2 France 0.

1964:   **First round**
First round: East Germany 2 Czechoslovakia 1;
Czechoslovakia 1 East Germany 1.

1968-72: **Eliminated in qualifying tournament**
1976:   **Winners**
Quarter-final: Czechoslovakia 2 Soviet Union 0;
Soviet Union 2 Czechoslovakia 2.
Semi-final: Czechoslovakia 3 Holland 1 (aet).
Final: Czechoslovakia 2 West Germany 2 (5-3 pen.)

1980:   **Third**
Group One: West Germany 1 Czechoslvakia 0;
Czechoslovakia 3 Greece 1;
Czechoslovakia 1 Holland 1.
Third-place play-off: Czechoslovakia 1 Italy 1 (9-8 pens)

1984-92: **Eliminated in qualifying tournament**

Italy

Strip:
Blue shirts, white shorts, blue socks
Change:
White shirts, blue shorts, white socks

Coach:
Arrigo Sacchi

FIFA world ranking:
3

There is no doubt that Italy possess more than enough talent to win the European Championship – any team that can deem Roberto Baggio surplus to requirements must be in with a shout. But if they are to have any chance of taking their second European Championship, Italy cannot afford to make the kind of slow start which was such a feature of both their 1994 World Cup finals campaign and their Euro '96 qualifying matches. In a group as hard as this, there is little or no margin for recovery.

It only seems like a month or two ago that, through a series of gutsy performances and flourishes of inspiration, chiefly from Baggio, Italy reached the final of the World Cup only to lose out on penalties to Brazil. That they had reached the final at all was something of a miracle. They lost their opening game to the Republic of Ireland; then, against Norway, they faced another crisis when goalkeeper Gianluca Pagliuca was sent off. To bring on his reserve goalkeeper, Luca Marchegiani, coach Arrigo Sacchi decided, astonishingly, to bring off Roberto Baggio, his one acknowledged match-winner. However, against all the odds, Dino Baggio scored and despite being effectively reduced to nine men after Paolo Maldini's thigh injury left him a virtual spectator, the Italians bravely held on.

A scrambled draw against Mexico took them to a second-round meeting with Nigeria where, at 1-0 down, with two minutes to go and again reduced to ten men following Zola's dismissal for the mildest of challenges, Roberto Baggio slid a low shot just inside the post to take the game into extra time. Having looked dead on their feet, Italy were now the more composed thanks, no doubt, to the high-pressure atmosphere they experience each week. They claimed their narrowly deserved winner from the penalty spot. It was Roberto Baggio again who stole in with a late clincher against Spain in the next round and he became the match-winner for a third time when he scored twice against Bulgaria in the semi-final.

Throughout the tournament, Sacchi had received a barrage of abuse and criticism from the Italian press, but the former Milan coach knows that it comes with the territory. Since he took charge in 1991, Italy have lost only a handful of games (six up to the end of 1995) and reached the World Cup final, but he still has to put up with criticism back home.

His record notwithstanding, then, Sacchi must have wondered if his time was up when Italy opened their European Championship campaign with only four points from their first three games – included a disastrous defeat by Croatia in Palermo – and were in danger of not making the final tournament for the second successive time. However, they rediscovered their winning ways and were in dominant form in their remaining matches. Six wins and a 1-1 draw away to Croatia drew unexpected praise from the media, who appreciated that here was a team that was as resolute as ever, well organized but exciting to watch at the same time.

Sacchi was frequently censured for the number of players he was trying out (eighty-two candidates received squad call-ups in forty-four games), but he now appears to have a settled side which will probably include Angelo Perruzi as first-choice goalkeeper, Paolo Maldini at left back, Antonio Benarrivo at right back and Ciro Ferrara and Luigi Appoloni in central defence. Demetrio Albertini has developed into a true playmaker and is likely to be partnered in central midfield by Roberto di Matteo with either Dino Baggio, Stefano Eranio or Angelo di Livio on the midfield flanks. In attack, Fabrizio Ravanelli, Alessandro del Piero and Gianfranco Zola would probably be selected ahead of even Roberto Baggio and Giuseppe Senori.

Del Pierro, the new star of Italian football, could be the revelation of the tournament. An injury to Roberto Baggio allowed him into the Juventus side last season and he was a major factor in Juve's league title victory. He was such a natural replacement for Baggio that the club were not too worried when Baggio left to join Milan.

Zola will be keen to make his mark in a major tournament. The twenty-nine-year-old was the top scorer in qualifying and is a brilliantly creative player for both Parma and the national team. Essentially, he plays just in front of the midfield and uses his excellent vision and awareness to release team-mates with perfectly weighted passes. He is a deceptively strong runner on the ball, a tenacious tackler and strikes so well with both feet that he is probably the best free-kick specialist in Europe, if not the world.

A subject which still causes heated debate is the case of Gianluca Vialli, one of Italy's most popular strikers who was in outstanding form last season but failed to get a call-up for the national team. Vialli's last international appearance was in December 1992, but a slump in form and then an injury left him sidelined. No one could ignore his claims following his goalscoring achievements and leadership qualities for Juventus once he had returned to fitness and in September 1995 Sacchi announced that it was time for Vialli to be recalled. Unfortunately, the coach also let it be known that he had come to this decision following consultation with players in the squad, a situation which Vialli found incredible and unacceptable. And he made his feelings clear. It is highly unlikely that he will ever play for his country again.

There is no denying that Italy reached the final of the World Cup without ever really playing at their best. Now, after all the experimentation, Sacchi has put together a side that boasts first-class and often world-class players in every position. If they do hit the right collective note, Italy could prove to be the most irresistible team in the competition, and Sacchi may silence his critics for once.

HOW THEY QUALIFIED

GROUP FOUR	P	W	D	L	F	A	PTS
Croatia	10	7	2	1	22	5	23
Italy	10	7	2	1	20	6	23
Lithuania	10	5	1	4	13	12	16
Ukraine	10	4	1	5	11	15	13
Slovenia	10	3	2	5	13	13	11
Estonia	10	0	0	10	3	31	0

Estonia 0 Croatia 2; Slovenia 1 **Italy 1**; Ukraine 0 Lithuania 2;
Croatia 2 Lithuania 0; Estonia 0 **Italy 2**; Ukraine 0 Slovenia 0;
Ukraine 3 Estonia 0; Slovenia 1 Lithuania 2; **Italy 1** Croatia 2;
Italy 4 Estonia 1; Croatia 4 Ukraine 0; Slovenia 3 Estonia 0;
Ukraine 0 **Italy 2**; Lithuania 0 Croatia 0; Lithuania 0 **Italy 1**;
Croatia 2 Slovenia 0; Estonia 0 Ukraine 1; Lithuania 2 Slovenia 1;
Estonia 1 Slovenia 3; Ukraine 1 Croatia 0; Estonia 0 Lithuania 1;
Croatia 7 Estonia 1; **Italy 1** Slovenia 0; Lithuania 1 Ukraine 3;
Croatia 1 **Italy 1**; Slovenia 3 Ukraine 2; Lithuania 5 Estonia 0;
Italy 3 Ukraine 1; Slovenia 1 Croatia 2; **Italy 4** Lithuania 0.

PAST PERFORMANCE IN EUROPEAN CHAMPIONSHIP FINALS

Best performance: Winners 1968.

Italy won the European Championship in 1968 but only after their goalless semi-final with the Soviet Union had been decided on the toss of a coin. They then had to survive a superb display by Yugoslavia to hold them to a 1-1 draw before beating them in the replay 2-0.

Although Italy reached the final of the World Cup in 1970 and won the trophy in 1982, such success was not forthcoming in the European Championship. They failed to qualify in 1976 and then as hosts in 1980 they played out two 0-0 draws against Spain and Belgium and beat England 1-0 for the dubious honour of competing in the third-place play-off, which they eventually lost 9-8 on penalties to Czechoslovakia.

For the 1988 championships, new coach Azeglio Vicini had started the process of rebuilding following a poor showing in the 1986 World Cup. He had drafted in members of the Under-21 side alongside more experienced players, and although Italy's priority was to develop a World Cup-winning side in time for 1990, when they would host the tournament, they reached the semi-finals, where they lost to an uncompromising Soviet side.

1960: Did not enter
1964: Second round
    First round: Italy 6 Turkey 0; Turkey 0 Italy 1.
    Second round: Soviet Union 2 Italy 0; Italy 1 Soviet Union 1.
1968: Winners
    Quarter-final: Bulgaria 3 Italy 2; Italy 2 Bulgaria 0.
    Semi-final: Italy 0 Soviet Union 0 (Italy won on toss of coin).
    Final: Italy 1 Yugoslavia 1. Replay: Italy 2 Yugoslavia 0.
1972: Quarter-finalists
    Italy 0 Belgium 0; Belgium 2 Italy 0.
1976: Eliminated in qualifying tournament
1980: Fourth
    Group Two: Italy 0 Spain 0; Italy 1 England 0;
    Italy 0 Belgium 0.
    Third-place play-off: Czechoslovakia 1 Italy 1 (9-8 pens)
1984: Eliminated in qualifying tournament
1988: Semi-finalists
    Group One: West Germany 1 Italy 1; Italy 1 Spain 0;
    Italy 2 Denmark 0. Semi-final: Soviet Union 2 Italy 0.
1992: Eliminated in qualifying tournament

Russia

Strip:
White shirts, blue shorts, white socks
Change:
Red shirts, white shorts, red socks

Coach:
Oleg Romantsev

FIFA world ranking:
5

Not even Oleg Salenko's record five goals in one game could over-come the fact that Russia's first World Cup appearance in their own right had been a huge disppointment. The 6-1 drubbing of Cameroon had come too late – there had already been defeats at the hands of Brazil and Sweden – but, in truth, Russia's problems had started before the 1994 finals had even begun.

Shortly after they qualified for the World Cup finals, a number of Russian players had signed an open letter threatening to withdraw from the national squad unless manager Pavel Sadyrin was replaced by Anatoli Bishovets, the former national coach. They considered Sadyrin's tactics old-fashioned and, to complicate matters further, there was also a dispute over money and poor training facilities. The Russian federa-tion supported Sadyrin's position, and as a result some of Russia's finest players removed themselves from the squad.

The team that faced Brazil in their opening match of the finals was clearly dispirited, and without five of their first-class players they could offer only a token challenge to the eventual winners. Defeat in their second game at the hands of Sweden effectively ended Russia's hopes of progressing to the second round – a sad end for a team with such a proud tradition in major tournaments.

In August 1994, by popular demand, Sadyrin was replaced by former Spartak Moscow coach Oleg Romantsev, who immediately restored Andrei Kanchelskis, Igor Shalimov, Vasili Koulkov and Igor Kolyvanov, among others, to the international team in readiness for the European

Championship qualifiers.

It cannot be denied that Russia were drawn in one of the easier groups, but their superiority was never in question. The only team to provide any sort of resistance to their inexorable progress was Scotland, who earned two hard-fought draws. Russia simply brushed their other group rivals aside. Greece, who had qualified from the same group as Russia for the World Cup finals, were beaten 3-0 at home and it was left to the Faroe Isles to provide the one moment of light relief when they took a 2-1 lead at home before eventually succumbing to constant Russian pressure and losing 5-2. Their twenty-six points and thirty-four goals scored to just five conceded was a record that no other participating country with the exception of Spain could touch.

In December, Romantsev quit his post as coach of Moscow Spartak to concentrate all his efforts on preparing the national team for the European Championship finals. He has been a key figure in the development of the Russian game ever since taking charge of Spartak in 1989 and both club and national team play a fluid game which follows the total-football approach more closely than any Russian system of the past.

There is every chance that Romantsev will rely heavily on a mix of ex-pats and Moscow Spartak players for the national squad. Moscow Spartak has emerged as the dominant force in Russian club football and is packed with internationals. They were the only club to win all their games in the Champions League but tempting offers from foreign clubs have already lured away some of their key players. One of the most significant departures was that of Viktor Onopko, Russia's Player of the Year in 1992, who got himself into a right old mess of a contract war between Real Oviedo and Atletico Madrid, both of whom felt they had a claim on his services. FIFA eventually ruled that while both clubs had negotiated contracts with the Russian midfielder it was Oviedo who had priority rights.

Romantsev's concerns that other players might accept similar offers were justified when striker Sergei Yuran, who scored the decisive goal against Blackburn Rovers at Ewood Park in the Champions League, and midfielder Vasili Kulkov both joined Millwall on loan until the end of the season. The two Russian internationals had only returned to Moscow Spartak from Porto a matter of months before making the move.

One player going the other way is goalkeeper Stanislav Cherchesov, who rejoined Moscow Spartak from Dynamo Dresden. It will be an ideal opportunity for him to build up an understanding with his defenders, Dmitri Khlestov and Yuri Nikiforov and with Russian Player of the year Ilia Tsimbilar, who formed the heart of the club's defence with Onopko before the latter moved to Spain. The twenty-six-year-old international is considered a potential top-class player by many and was instrumental in Russia's success in two key European qualifying games, against Finland and Greece.

Tsimbilar will be joined in midfield by the cultured playmaker Valeri Karpin, who is the creative heart of Russia's attacking moves. There is a wealth of options and plenty of pace up front, with Foggia's Kolyvanov, who was top scorer in the qualifiers, Kiriakov, Shalimov, Radchenko, Yuran and Kanchelskis all battling for a place in the team.

The former Soviet Union have a long and distinguished pedigree in this competition, having won the first tournament and finished runners-up three times – a record second only to Germany's. With the rebels back on board, this Russian team is in good shape to continue the tradition.

HOW THEY QUALIFIED

GROUP EIGHT	P	W	D	L	F	A	PTS
Russia	10	8	2	0	34	5	26
Scotland	10	7	2	1	19	3	23
Greece	10	6	0	4	23	9	18
Finland	10	5	0	5	18	18	15
Faroe Isles	10	2	0	8	10	35	6
San Marino	10	0	0	10	2	36	0

Finland 0 Scotland 2; Faroe Isles 1 Greece 5; Scotland 5 Faroe Isles 1; Greece 4 Finland 0; **Russia 4** San Marino 0; Scotland 1 **Russia 1**; Greece 2 San Marino 0; Finland 5 Faroe Isles 0; Finland 4 San Marino 1; Greece 1 Scotland 0; **Russia 0** Scotland 0; San Marino 0 Finland 2; San Marino 0 Scotland 2; Greece 0 **Russia 3**; Faroe Isles 0 Finland 4; **Russia 3** Faroe Isles 0; Faroe Isles 3 San Marino 0; Faroe Isles 0 Scotland 2; San Marino 0 **Russia 7**; Finland 2 Greece 1; Scotland 1 Greece 0; Finland 0 **Russia 6**; Scotland 1 Finland 0; Faroe Isles 2 **Russia 5**; San Marino 0 Greece 4; **Russia 2** Greece 1; San Marino 1 Faroe Isles 3; Scotland 5 San Marino 0; **Russia 3** Finland 1; Greece 5 Faroe Isles 0.

PAST PERFORMANCE IN EUROPEAN CHAMPIONSHIP FINALS
(as the Soviet Union)

Best performance: Winners 1960

The former Soviet Union has one of the best records in the European Championship. They reached three of the first four finals and lost a 1968 semi-final on the toss of a coin to Italy. Their only victory, though, was in the inaugural Nations Cup in 1960, when they beat Yugoslavia 2-1 in the final. They lost the 1964 final 2-1 to Spain and the 1972 decider 3-0 to Germany. After their defeat in the quarter-finals to the eventual champions, Czechoslovakia, in 1976, they went into decline, failing to qualify for the next two championships. They bounced back in 1988 to reach the final in Munich, where they lost 2-0 to the Dutch team they had beaten 1-0 in an earlier group match.

1960: **Winners**
First round: Soviet Union 3 Hungary 1; Hungary 0
Soviet Union 1.
Quarter-final: Soviet Union v Spain Soviet Union walked
over as Spain withdrew.
Semi-final: Soviet Union 3 Czechoslovakia 0.
Final: Soviet Union 2 Yugoslavia 1 (aet).

1964: **Runners-up**
First round: bye. Second round: Soviet Union 2 Italy 0;
Italy 1 Soviet Union 1.
Quarter-final: Sweden 1 Soviet Union 1;
Soviet Union 3 Sweden 1.
Semi-final: Soviet Union 3 Denmark 0.
Final: Spain 2 Soviet Union 1.

1968: **Fourth**
Quarter-final: Hungary 2 Soviet Union 0;
Soviet Union 3 Hungary 0.
Semi-final: Italy 0 Soviet Union 0 (Italy won on coin toss).
Third-place play-off: England 2 Soviet Union 0.

1972: **Runners-up**
Quarter-final: Yugoslavia 0 Soviet Union 0;
Soviet Union 3 Yugoslavia 0.
Semi-final: Soviet Union 1 Hungary 0.
Final: West Germany 3 Soviet Union 0.

1976: **Quarter-finalists**
Quarter-final: Czechoslovakia 2 Soviet Union 0;
Soviet Union 2 Czechoslovakia 2.

1980-84: **Eliminated in qualifying tournament**
1988: **Runners-up**
Group Two: Soviet Union 1 Holland 0; Soviet Union 1
Republic of Ireland 1; Soviet Union 3 England 1.
Semi-final: Soviet Union 2 Italy 0.
Final: Holland 2 Soviet Union 0.

1992: **First round**
Germany 1 CIS 1; Holland 0 CIS 0; Scotland 3 CIS 0.

Group D

Denmark, Portugal, Turkey, Croatia

No team has ever won two consecutive European Championships, and, as marvellous as their win four years ago was, it's difficult to see Denmark repeating the feat that saw them beat France, Holland and then Germany in a thrilling final in 1992.

As holders, Denmark are the seeded team in the group but they are by no means the favourites to qualify for a place in the quarter-finals. That distinction is shared by Croatia and Portugal, who both won their qualifying groups with something to spare. Denmark finished second to Spain in one of the tougher groups while Turkey came second in Group Three having beaten top-of-the-table Switzerland and World Cup semi-finalists Sweden, along the way.

The first game of the group will tell us a lot about whether Portugal are serious contenders as outright winners of the tournament. They have impressed many people with their fluid style, while their exceptionally talented midfield of Paulo Sousa, Rui Costa and Luis Figo is one of the best in the world. But there must be a question-mark over them for their lack of major championship experience and Denmark are the sort of team that can expose any weaknesses. Yet, twelve years ago, Denmark were in a similar position themselves, and reached the semi-finals of the European Championship and the second round of the 1986 World Cup with some refreshingly entertaining football. Insufficient big-match experience is unlikely to be a problem for many of the Portuguese players individually as a good number of them are involved in top-level club football in Italy's Serie A, Spain or their own hard domestic league every week. However, it is a factor worth considering in the context of the team as a whole.

This is Croatia's first appearance in the finals and the way they won their qualifying group suggests that they will progress further. Turkey are certainly not to be underestimated, but Croatia should make their first game a winning one if they continue the improvement that saw them beat Italy 2-1 in Palermo with goals from Davor Suker.

By the time the Portuguese come to play Croatia on 19 June, each side should have done enough to have already confirmed qualification for the next stage if either of them are to move on.

Denmark v Portugal	9 June, 7.30 pm, Hillsborough	**BBC**
Turkey v Croatia	11 June, 7.30 pm, City Ground	**ITV**
Portugal v Turkey	14 June, 4.30 pm, City Ground	**BBC**
Croatia v Denmark	16 June, 6.00 pm, Hillsborough	**BBC**
Croatia v Portugal	19 June, 4.30 pm, City Ground	**ITV**
Turkey v Denmark	19 June, 4.30 pm, Hillsborough	**ITV**

Denmark

Strip:
Red shirts, white shorts, red socks
Change:
All white

Coach:
Richard Moller Nielsen

FIFA world ranking:
10

Even Steven Spielberg would have dismissed as 'far-fetched' the tale of a football team being hastily recalled from their holiday to take part in a major competition in which they come close to defeat before going on to beat the European champions and, in a thrilling finale, overcome the reigning world champions. Nobody would believe it: in modern sport, fairytales just don't happen. But this one did, and Denmark's extraordinary performances against their much-vaunted opponents owed everything to tireless teamwork and spirit and they fully deserved, in this expanded sixteen-team championship, an automatic place as the holders.

Instead, Denmark were forced to qualify, and from one of the more tricky groups at that. While Spain were romping away at the head of the table, the Danes were involved in a tight battle with Belgium. In their first game, Denmark, disappointingly, drew away to Macedonia but they amended matters with an important 3-1 home win over Belgium before losing to runaway leaders Spain by 3-0. As if to prove that Denmark were not the only giant-killers around, Cyprus then held them to a 1-1 draw, a result which left four teams in equal second place. The crucial game was always going to be the return tie in Belgium, and thanks to a gift goal and some excellent goalkeeping from Peter Schmeichel, Denmark were the winners by 3-1.

This game saw another great performance from the enormously talented Michael Laudrup, who missed out on Denmark's great European Championship triumph because he refused to play for his country while Richard Moller Nielsen was in charge. Last season Laudrup ended a fantastic career at Barcelona and moved to arch-rivals Real Madrid, whom he helped to win the Spanish title.

Denmark ensured qualification with a 1-1 home draw against Spain which was marked by a crucial equalizer from the hero of 1992, Kim Vilfort, who had just recovered from a back injury.

When Denmark got the call-up to the 1992 championship Richard Moller Nielsen had just two weeks to prepare his side. This time he has had the comparative luxury of seven months in which to organize his team and tactics. He has done so in the knowledge that these will be his last games in charge of the national team. After the finals he will start as manager of Finland, the one country in the region not to have made the finals of a major tournament.

Moller Nielsen is a shrewd coach and created a wonderful team spirit four years ago. This time he has put together a younger team. They will rely heavily on Schmeichel's hugely influential presence, both physical and mental, in goal and on sweeper Jes Hogh in defence. There is a core of players from Brondby – who beat Liverpool in the UEFA Cup – including Vilfort, goalkeeper Mogens Krogh, Jens Risager and midfielder Allan Nielsen, who scored an astonishing debut goal in the 2-0 away win over Armenia. Shortly after going on as a substitute, replacing John Jensen, he sprinted down the wing and crossed the ball straight into the net. Great things are expected of him.

The other rising star is Mikkel Beck, who plays for Rangers. He scored three goals in six internationals and has been compared to that other great Danish striker Preben Elkjaer. If he's even remotely as talented as that formidable player he will be very good, and prob-ably the best man to judge is Michael Laudrup who played alongside Elkjaer in the wonderful Danish side of the early eighties onwards.

Michael Laudrup, who has apparently patched up his differences with the coach, could form a useful partnership in attack with his brother Brian, who possesses the same close control and vision. It is a bitter shame that the Danes will be without Fleming Polvsen, whose tireless running up front exemplified his country's unselfish attitude four years ago.

HOW THEY QUALIFIED

GROUP TWO	P	W	D	L	F	A	PTS
Spain	10	8	2	0	25	4	26
Denmark	10	6	3	1	19	9	21
Belgium	10	4	3	3	17	12	15
Macedonia	10	1	4	5	9	18	7
Cyprus	10	1	4	5	6	20	7
Armenia	10	1	2	7	5	17	5

Cyprus 1 Spain 2; Macedonia 1 **Denmark 1**; Belgium 2 Armenia 0; Armenia 0 Cyprus 0; **Denmark 3** Belgium 1; Macedonia 0 Spain 2; Belgium 1 Macedonia 1; Spain 3 **Denmark 0**; Cyprus 2 Armenia 0; Belgium 1 Spain 4; Macedonia 3 Cyprus 0; Spain 1 Belgium 1; Cyprus 1 **Denmark 1**; Armenia 0 Spain 2; Belgium 2 Cyprus 0; **Denmark 1** Macedonia 0; Armenia 2 Macedonia 2; **Denmark 4** Cyprus 0; Macedonia 0 Belgium 5; Spain 1 Armenia 0; Armenia 0 **Denmark 2**; Belgium 1 **Denmark 3**; Spain 6 Cyprus 0; Macedonia 1 Armenia 2; Armenia 0 Belgium 2; **Denmark 1** Spain 1; Cyprus 1 Macedonia 1; Spain 3 Macedonia 0; **Denmark 3** Armenia 1; Cyprus 1 Belgium 1.

PAST PERFORMANCE IN EUROPEAN CHAMPIONSHIP FINALS

Best performance: Winners 1992

Denmark maintained a strict amateur code for many years and footballers playing for foreign clubs were not allowed to represent their country. When this ban was finally lifted in 1976 the national side was quick to make its mark. Players such as Preben Elkjaer, Michael Laudrup, Morten Olsen and Soren Lerby were the heart of the team that reached the 1984 European Championship finals. They lost narrowly to the eventual winners, France, and beat Yugoslavia 5-0 in the group games, but lost on penalties to Spain in the semi-finals. They won a lot of admirers for their exciting brand of football and it encouraged development in the domestic game, from which a new generation of players emerged to sensationally win the 1992 European Championship in Sweden.

1960:   **First round**
Denmark 2 Czechoslovakia 2;
Czechoslovakia 5 Denmark 1.

1964:   **Fourth**
First round: Denmark 6 Malta 1; Malta 1 Denmark 3.
Second round: Denmark 4 Albania 0;
Albania 1 Denmark 0.
Quarter-final: Luxembourg 3 Denmark 3;
Denmark 2 Luxembourg 2;
Denmark 1 Luxembourg 0 (Amsterdam).
Semi-final: Soviet Union 3 Denmark 0.
Third-place play-off: Hungary 3 Denmark 1.

1968-80: Eliminated in qualifying tournament

1984:   **Semi-finalists**
Group One: France 1 Denmark 0;
Denmark 5 Yugoslavia 0; Denmark 3 Belgium 2.
Semi-final: Spain 1 Denmark 1 (5 - 4 pens).

1988:   **First round**
Group One: Spain 3 Denmark 2;
West Germany 2 Denmark 0; Italy 2 Denmark 0.

1992:   **Winners**
Group One: Denmark 0 England 0;
Sweden 1 Denmark 0; Denmark 2 France 1.
Semi-final: Denmark 2 Holland 2 (5-4 pens).
Final: Denmark 2 Germany 0.

Portugal

Strip:
Red shirts, green shorts, red socks
Change:
White shirts, dark red shorts, green socks

Coach:
Antonio Ribeiro de Oliveira

FIFA world ranking:
16

Even today, football in Portugal is intimately associated with one out-standing player: Eusebio. He was a vital ingredient in the huge success of Portuguese football at both club and international level throughout the 1960s, when Benfica competed in five European Cup finals, winning two of them, and Portugal reached the semi-final of the 1966 World Cup. But this record only highlights the fact that for thirty years the Portuguese have struggled to live up to the reputation of those teams.

Portugal is sorely in need of a contemporary footballing success story, and in the current squad, which qualified so impressively from Group Six, they have a team which is among the very best in Europe, and one that could rival the performances of the 1966 World Cup side.

The team is a fascinating blend of experience and youthful talent, the result of a long and careful programme of grass-roots develop-ment which saw Portugal win the 1989 and 1991 World Youth Cups. Since then, members of those youth teams such as Paulo Sousa, Rui Costa, Fernanado Couto and Luis Figo have progressed to play for some of Europe's biggest clubs and have formed the creative heart of a fast-maturing national side brimming with ability.

Portugal stormed through to qualify for their first major tourna-ment in twelve years with an ease which belied four successive failures at world and European level. Opening victories away to Northern Ireland and Latvia were followed by a comfortable 1-0 home win over Austria – the result did not do justice to Portugal's superiority. They hammered Lichtenstein by 8-0 but lost their first game of the competition to an own goal – by goalkeeper Vitor Baia – against the Republic of Ireland.

A home victory over Latvia was needed to renew the momentum. Goals from Figo, Carlos Secretario and Domingos Oliveira – Portugal's leading scorer in the qualifiers – were sufficient to take them back to the top, where they were to remain. They put another seven past Lichtenstein in August but found goals hard to come by in their next two games, against Northern Ireland at home and away to Austria, and had to settle for two 1-1 draws. The Portuguese dominated for long spells in both games but were unable to finish their excellent approach work.

By this time, the Republic of Ireland's challenge had slipped away in the face of two defeats against an average Austrian side, and when they travelled to Lisbon on the night of the final group games their priority was holding on to their second-place position. The Irish needed a result to make sure of avoiding the play-off, but instead Portugal put on a second-half display which tore the Irish defence apart in a way no other team had managed for many years. In driving rain, Ireland survived the early onslaught, but then in the fifty-ninth minute, the most beautiful, inch-perfect lob from Rui Costa from 25 yards opened the scoring and the floodgates. Helder met Folha's corner with a stooping header and Cadete rounded off an emphatic win in the final minutes. In terms of fitness, technique and the way the game was played, the Portuguese had outclassed their opponents.

Now comes the hard part. Qualifying is one thing, but do the talented youngsters have the experience and ability to succeed in a major competition? They have been drawn in a group which gives them every chance and should have done enough by the time they meet their toughest group opponents, Croatia, to be safely through to the quarter-finals.

Vitor Baia is solid in goal while Paulinho Santos and Couto, who plays for Parma, form a tight defensive unit. But it is the midfield trio of whom so much is expected. In Costa, Sousa and Figo, the Portuguese have a midfield of sublime gifts. Each of them possesses a glorious touch and produces runs and passes which stretch their opponents. Costa, a former member of Portugal's World Youth Cup champions, was just twenty-two when he was transferred from Benfica to the Italian club Fiorentina for £5 million. A creative, play-making midfielder, he is one of the reasons why Gabriel Batistuta scored a club record twenty-six goals last season for Fiorentina. The Argentinian striker was provided with superbly timed balls and the silver service has continued this season.

Paulo Sousa also made a stunning impact in Italian football when he moved to Juventus from Sporting Lisbon in 1994. The twenty-six-year-old had a brilliant season and, along with Gianluca Vialli, Fabrizio Ravanelli and Ciro Ferrara, he was instrumental in winning Juve their first Scudetta since 1986. In a survey by an Italian weekly sports paper he was voted as one of the three best players in Serie A last season. Sousa possesses excellent awareness and vision and controls the midfield with precise passes, always alive to the opportunity to release his front men. He doesn't score many goals himself, but he creates them for others.

The third member of the trio, Figo, plays for Barcelona in a midfield which also boasts the talents of Gheorge Hagi and Robert Prosinecki. Figo has chipped in with a number of crucial goals for Portugal during qualification, and while Sousa provides the anchor, Figo pushes forward with Costa leaving the experienced Oceano to play a bit deeper.

If there is a weakness in the Portuguese side, it is their inability to put chances away after promising approach play. Coach Antonio Oliveira has probably one of the best midfields in Europe, if not the world, and must rue the absence of world-class striker Paulo Futre, who could convert the wealth of goalscoring opportunities provided by Costa and co. Since moving to Reggiana in 1993, and subsequently to Milan last year, Futre, who was only seventeen when he made his international debut, has been kept out by a series of injuries and it must be doubtful whether the skilful thirty-year-old winger will recover in time to lend his undoubted talent to the national cause.

Domingos finished as Portugal's top scorer in the qualifying stages with six, but Paulo Alves, with five, took his chance against England very well, thumping a first-time shot past David Seaman after some wonderful approach play. This was after England had taken the lead in the wake of Steve Stone's excellent strike, but it should be remembered that Portugal were without Costa and neither Figo nor Sousa reappeared for the second half. Although the game finished 1-1, the Portuguese demonstrated a speed and flexibility of movement that was exciting to watch. They were able to change their positions without affecting their fluency and supported their strikers with runs from a variety of deep positions.

Portugal have the ability to go far in the tournament. The only doubt must centre on their lack of big-tournament experience.

HOW THEY QUALIFIED

GROUP SIX	P	W	D	L	F	A	PTS
Portugal	10	7	2	1	29	7	23
Republic of Ireland	10	5	2	3	17	11	17
Northern Ireland	10	5	2	3	20	15	17
Austria	10	5	1	4	29	14	16
Latvia	10	4	0	6	11	20	12
Liechtenstein	10	0	1	9	1	40	1

Northern Ireland 4 Liechtenstein 1; Liechtenstein 0 Austria 4;
Northern Ireland 1 **Portugal 2**; Latvia 0 Republic of Ireland 3;
Latvia 1 **Portugal 3**; Austria 1 Northern Ireland 2; Republic of Ireland 4
Liechtenstein 0; **Portugal 1** Austria 0; Liechtenstein 0 Latvia 1;
Northern Ireland 0 Republic of Ireland 4; **Portugal 8** Liechtenstein 0;
Republic of Ireland 1 Northern Ireland 1; Austria 5 Latvia 0;
Republic of Ireland 1 **Portugal 0**; Latvia 0 Northern Ireland 1;
Austria 7 Liechtenstein 0; **Portugal 3** Latvia 2; Liechtenstein 0
Republic of Ireland 0; Northern Ireland 1 Latvia 2; Republic of Ireland 1
Austria 3; Liechtenstein 0 **Portugal 7**; Latvia 3 Austria 2;
Portugal 1 Northern Ireland 1; Austria 3 Republic of Ireland 1;
Latvia 1 Liechtenstein 0; Republic of Ireland 2 Latvia 1; Austria 1
Portugal 1; Liechtenstein 0 Northern Ireland 4; **Portugal 3**
Republic of Ireland 0; Northern Ireland 5 Austria 3.

PAST PERFORMANCE IN EUROPEAN CHAMPIONSHIP FINALS

Best performance: Semi-finalists 1984

Reaching the last four in 1984 remains Portugal's sole significant contribution to the European Championship finals. They drew both their opening games and qualified for the semis by virtue of Nene's goal against Romania. They then produced their best football against France with Chalana, in particular, a constant threat. Their 2-1 lead took Portugal to within six minutes of a place in the final, but first Domergue, then Platini, saved the game for the French.

1960:   **Quarter-finalists**
First round: Portugal 3 East Germany 2;
East Germany 0 Portugal 2.
Quarter-final: Portugal 2 Yugoslavia 1;
Yugoslavia 5 Portugal 1.

1964:   **First round**
Bulgaria 3 Portugal 1; Portugal 3 Bulgaria 1; Bulgaria 1 Portugal 0 (Rome).

1968-80: **Eliminated in qualifying tournament**

1984:   **Semi-finalists**
Group Two: Portugal 0 West Germany 0;
Portugal 1 Spain 1; Portugal 1 Romania 0.
Semi-final: France 3 Portugal 2 (aet).

1988-92: **Eliminated in qualifying tournament**

Turkey

Strip:
All white with red trim
Change:
Red shirts, white shorts, red socks

Coach:
Fatih Terim

FIFA world ranking:
31

It has long been a mystery why Turkey hasn't developed into a top European football nation much sooner: they have a population of nearly 60 million, support verging on the fanatical, and no lack of talented players. A solitary appearance in the World Cup finals in 1954 seems a poor return for a country boasting such potential.

So, after a series of foreign coaches had failed to lead Turkey into the finals of a major international championship, it was somewhat ironic that they should qualify for this one under the guidance of a Turkish coach, Fatih Terim. Hailed as the saviour of Turkish football, the forty-two-year-old ex-international must take an enormous amount of credit for transforming the national side.

Terim took over as national coach from Sepp Piontek in 1993 after Turkey had failed to qualify for the World Cup. He had spent several years working with Piontek and was well aware that the country possessed many talented players at senior and particularly youth level, where he was the under-21 coach. Terim, who had played in a record fifty-one internationals for his country, set about motivating a fighting spirit and fierce will to win in his team, a quality he felt had been lacking under previous managers. He wanted players who would compete and be prepared to chase lost causes, and radically changed the team around. Terim's philosophy was tested in their first European qualifying game against Hungary. Turkey came back from 2-0 down with goals from Hakan Suker and Bulent Uygun to claim a well-earned point.

Following their 5-0 win over Iceland, Turkey lost to visitors Switzerland and faced another stiff task at home to Sweden, who had finished third in the World Cup. This was to be a severe test of the Turks' new-found resilience, but despite conceding an early goal, Terim's team came back to win 2-1 – a great result given the pressure of the situation. Terim even left out Turkey's captain and most experienced player, Oguz, for the start of game. His judgement was again vindicated when Oguz delivered a superb performance after coming on as a second-half substitute.

That victory moved Turkey up into second place in the table. The optimism surrounding the national team grew to fever pitch in April, when they inflicted on Switzerland their first defeat at home since 1992, by 2-1. The dream of qualifying moved even closer when, in September, Turkey beat Hungary for the first time since 1956. Two goals by Hakan Suker marked a fine display by the young striker, although for some reason he was booked for pulling off his shirt while celebrating the second. His two headers took his tally to thirteen international goals, only eight short of that of Turkey's all-time leading scorer, Lefter Kuckandonyadis, who had also scored twice against Hungary, in the famous 1956 victory over a side that boasted Puskas, Bozsik and Czibor.

Hakan's skill and non-stop running had attracted the attention of foreign clubs and the tall striker became one of only a handful of Turkish stars to play his club football overseas when he moved from Galatasaray to Torino for around £2 million. However, the twenty-four-year-old claimed that he had not wanted to leave Turkey and that the deal had been arranged between club directors. After scoring one goal in five appearances for his new club it came as no surprise when Galatasaray agreed to pay Torino the same fee to bring him back home after five months.

Turkey had the chance of finishing top of the table but drew both remaining games, against Iceland and Sweden, and had to be content second place. They went through as the third-best qualifier of the teams that had finished second in their group. The Turks had needed at least a point from their game against Sweden in Stockholm to ensure that they avoided the play-off and although they were twice a goal down, they rallied back to earn a draw demonstrating their new-found resilience in the process.

Turkey's qualification was a personal success for Terim, who has

adopted a tighter system than his predecessors and will not be over-
awed by the occasion. Turkey now deploy a 3-4-2-1 system which
allows players to support the front men without leaving themselves
exposed at the back. Hakan is undoubtedly the star of the team and
will spearhead an attack which has two men out wide to provide the
sort of crosses the tall target man thrives on. The effectiveness of
Terim's method is illustrated by the fact that Turkey have scored in
every qualifying game bar one since he's been in charge. Other players which have featured strongly are sweeper Ogun Temizkanoglu and
Oguz, who has now broken his coach's record of international caps.

Turkey will have a lot of support and opponents who treat them
as lightweights could be in for a surprise. Realistically, however, they
must play at their very best in all three games in order to have any
chance of reaching the quarter-finals.

HOW THEY QUALIFIED

GROUP THREE	P	W	D	L	F	A	PTS
Switzerland	8	5	2	1	15	7	17
Turkey	8	4	3	1	16	8	15
Sweden	8	2	3	3	9	10	9
Hungary	8	2	2	4	7	13	8
Iceland	8	1	2	5	3	12	5

Iceland 0 Sweden 1; Hungary 2 **Turkey 2**; **Turkey 5** Iceland 0;
Switzerland 4 Sweden 2; Switzerland 1 Iceland 0; Sweden 2 Hungary 0;
Turkey 1 Switzerland 2; **Turkey 2** Sweden 1; Hungary 2
Switzerland 2; Hungary 1 Sweden 0; Switzerland 1 **Turkey 2**;
Sweden 1 Iceland 1; Iceland 2 Hungary 1; Iceland 0 Switzerland 2;
Sweden 0 Switzerland 0; **Turkey 2** Hungary 0; Switzerland 3
Hungary 0; Iceland 0 **Turkey 0**; Hungary 1 Iceland 0;
Sweden 2 **Turkey 2**.

PAST PERFORMANCE IN EUROPEAN CHAMPIONSHIP FINALS

Best performance: First round 1960, 1964.

Although they did not become members of UEFA until 1962, Turkey were invited to take part in the inaugural championship and were somewhat unlucky to lose out on goal difference to Romania. Since then, the national team has never got beyond the qualifying round, and although they have often proved tough to beat at home, they have been on the wrong end of some drubbings on their travels.

1960: First round
Romania 3 Turkey 0; Turkey 2 Romania 0.
1964: First round
Italy 6 Turkey 0; Turkey 0 Italy 1.
1968-92: Eliminated in qualifying tournament

Croatia

Strip:
Red and white checked shirts, white shorts, white socks
Change:
All white

Coach:
Otto Baric

FIFA World ranking:
41

Every team competing in the European Championship will be playing with a strong feeling of national pride but none, one suspects, will be more fiercely motivated than Croatia. For them, footballing success is an opportunity to raise the morale and realize the dreams of a war-weary population that has suffered the break up of their country.

Football is without doubt the most popular sport in a land which has produced highly skilled players and has often proved to be one of the most talented footballing nations. The problem has traditionally been one of nationalism, and even before the Yugoslavs were forced to withdraw from the 1992 European Championship, their Croatian members had already decided against playing for the collective national team.

Croatia now have their own side which, they believe, can challenge the very best. With players of the calibre of Zvonimir Boban, Davor Suker, Robert Prosinecki and Alen Boksic, and in the light of the sensational 2-1 victory over Italy in Palermo, few would question their belief. That performance was the highlight of an impressive qualification which saw them top the group table, forcing the World Cup runners-up, Italy, into second place.

However, delight at qualifying for the finals was soured by the national federation's decision to relieve Tomislav Ivic of his position as national team director. Ivic was in charge of team selection at all levels, with Miroslav Blazevic acting as coach to the senior squad.

Long before the process of qualifying for the finals began, Ivic and Blazevic had taken the unusual step of ruling that the players would not be paid for victories or points gained. Instead each player received £400 expenses for each match, and those who had taken part in all ten qualifying games were paid a £40,000 bonus. The players were only too happy to go along with this arrangement, which created a strong team spirit.

Although they hadn't always seen eye to eye – Ivic preferred long, careful preparations, Blazevic more experimental tactics – they had put together a squad of extremely gifted players. However, the federation decided that some comments Ivic made were counter-productive and brought in two other coaches alongside Blazevic, who, they believed, deserved most of the credit for the team's success.

If that were not enought disruption, Blazevic himself remains under investigation by the French authorities in connection with bribery and match-fixing allegations involving Marseille, and has already spent seventeen days in prison.

Otto Baric is the man most likely to succeed Blazevic as national coach. He will have at his disposal an outstanding team made up largely of foreign-based players. In a defence which conceded just five goals during qualification, Slaven Bilic is the first-choice central defender, partnering libero Nikola Jerkan. Robert Jarni, who helped Juventus to win the scudetto last year but who has since moved to Spain, is a quick left back who likes to get forward.

The heart, soul and captain of the team is Milan midfielder, Boban. He has donated thousands of pounds to aid organizations in his country and few Croatians will forget the day some six years ago when, outraged at seeing Serbian police attacking Croatian supporters at the Yugoslav Cup final between Red Star Belgrade and his team, Dinamo Zagreb, he was seen on TV retaliating with a kick at one of the officers. Boban moved to Milan in 1992 and has become an influential figure in the midfield for club and country with his surging runs and excellent distribution. He is joined in midfield by the sublimely talented Prosinecki, who won a Champions' Cup medal with Red Star Belgrade in 1991 before joining Real Madrid the following year. He has since moved to Barcelona, where the lack of regular first-team games has not been ideal preparation for the tournament.

If Boban is the inspiration in midfield, it is Suker who puts the chances away. He scored sixteen times in just fourteen internationals and was the qualifying round's top scorer for any country with twelve, including the two that stunned Italy in Palermo. He came late to prominence, despite having left Yugoslavia for Sevilla in 1991, but the twenty-eight-year-old has since become one of Europe's hottest goalscorers and was named player of the year in Croatia. His striking partner, Boksic, has yet to make such an impression as an international, although he is a powerful figure for Lazio.

Of those who continue to play in the domestic league, twenty-two-year-old Ivica Mornar of Hajduk Split is considered by many to be the most promising young striker in Croatia, while his club team-mate Milan Rapaic is one of the most talented. Each may have to wait their turn in such a gifted team.

HOW THEY QUALIFIED

GROUP FOUR	P	W	D	L	F	A	PTS
Croatia	10	7	2	1	22	5	23
Italy	10	7	2	1	20	6	23
Lithuania	10	5	1	4	13	12	16
Ukraine	10	4	1	5	11	15	13
Slovenia	10	3	2	5	13	13	11
Estonia	10	0	0	10	3	31	0

Estonia 0 **Croatia 2**; Slovenia 1 Italy 1; Ukraine 0 Lithuania 2; **Croatia 2** Lithuania 0; Estonia 0 Italy 2; Ukraine 0 Slovenia 0; Ukraine 3 Estonia 0; Slovenia 1 Lithuania 2; Italy 1 **Croatia 2**; Italy 4 Estonia 1; **Croatia 4** Ukraine 0; Slovenia 3 Estonia 0; Ukraine 0 Italy 2; Lithuania 0 **Croatia 0**; Lithuania 0 Italy 1; **Croatia 2** Slovenia 0; Estonia 0 Ukraine 1; Lithuania 2 Slovenia 1; Estonia 1 Slovenia 3; Ukraine 1 **Croatia 0**; Estonia 0 Lithuania 1; **Croatia 7** Estonia 1; Italy 1 Slovenia 0; Lithuania 1 Ukraine 3; **Croatia 1** Italy 1; Slovenia 3 Ukraine 2; Lithuania 5 Estonia 0; Italy 3 Ukraine 1; Slovenia 1 **Croatia 2**; Italy 4 Lithuania 0.

PAST PERFORMANCE IN EUROPEAN CHAMPIONSHIP FINALS
(As Yugoslavia)

This is Croatia's first appearance in the European Championship, through a unified country, Yugoslavia played in two of the first three finals, losing 2-1 after extra time to the Soviet Union in 1960 and 2-0 in a replay to the hosts Italy, in 1968.

Their best performance since then was to reach the semi-finals on home territory in 1976, where they lost 4-2 to Germany after extra time. They made only one appearance in the finals thereafter, when they lost all their group games in 1984 (which included a 5-0 drubbing by Denmark).

THE VENUES

BIRMINGHAM
Stadium: Villa Park
Host club: Aston Villa
Opened: 1897
Capacity: 40,000 for European Championship
Record: 76,558 v Derby County (1946)

MATCH SCHEDULE
Group A: Holland v Scotland 10 June 4.30 pm
Switzerland v Holland 13 June 7.30 pm
Scotland v Switzerland 18 June 7.30 pm
Quarter-final: 23 June 6.30 pm

Villa Park has a history of staging big games. It is one of three
European Championship club grounds that also hosted the 1966
World Cup and has become synonymous with FA Cup semi-finals. It
will host Group A games and a quarter-final for the European
Championship.

Aston Villa have been one of the most successful clubs in English
football since their foundation in 1874. It was one of their committee
members, William McGregor, who was instrumental in setting up a
football league and Villa became one of the founder clubs in 1888.
When they moved to Villa Park in 1897 they were in the middle of a
period of great success, winning five Division 1 championships

(1894, '96, '97, '99, 1900) and two FA Cups (1895, 1897), including the coveted league and cup double in 1897.

Naturally as the number of clubs and the standard of competition grew, the rate of Villa's success slowed and despite an FA Cup victory against Manchester United in 1957 and becoming the first winners of the League Cup in 1961, Villa's fortunes slumped as they sank to the third division. The arrival of Ron Saunders in 1975 revitalised the club. He restored the team to the first division and managed the club to two further League Cup wins, the league championship in 1981 and the European Cup the following year.

In addition to hosting Group Two World Cup fixtures in 1966, Villa Park is one of the most frequently used grounds for FA Cup semi-finals. Despite a £20 million redevelopment programme the stadium retains some of its traditional and famous look. The historic red brick main stand is still the centrepiece although it is somewhat over-shadowed by three modern stands, the North, Doug Ellis and the massive Holte End – the largest end stand in Britain.

LEEDS
Stadium: Elland Road
Host club: Leeds United
Capacity: 39,000 for European Championship
Record: 57,892

MATCH SCHEDULE
Group B: Spain v Bulgaria 9 June 2.30 pm
France v Spain 15 June 6.00 pm
Romania v Spain 18 June 4.30 pm

Where else will you get to see Hagi, Stoichkov and Cantona within the space of several days?

Like many other grounds, Elland Road has undergone a major remodernisation programme in recent years in the light of the Justice Taylor Report. The new East Stand cost six and a quarter million pounds when it was built in 1992/3 to replace the old Lowfields Road Stand. Seating 17,000 people, it is the largest cantilever stand in the world and boasts a concourse with shops, cafes and food outlets. The Revie Stand at the north end has developed over the years from what was once just a huge earth bank. It became a roofed terrace in 1968, nicknamed the Kop, but in 1994 this was replaced with the 7,000-seater Revie Stand, bringing the stadium in line with the all-seater regulation.

Leeds United FC, formed to replace Leeds City who were expelled from the league after claims of illegal payments, played their first league game at Elland Road in August 1920. United were relative latecomers to the Football League and their early history was one of modest achievement until the sixties.

The man responsible for making Leeds United a footballing power was Don Revie who joined the club in 1961 and stayed for 13 years. The former England forward transformed Leeds into a club which could consistently challenge for the major honours. In 1964 he took Leeds up from Division 2 and after finishing runners-up in the championship in 1965 and 1966 they beat Arsenal in a dour League Cup final in 1968 and also took the UEFA Cup against Ferencvaros.

The following year, Leeds landed their first League Championship by drawing at Liverpool with what was then a first division record of 67 points. Further honours followed as the side became the dominant force in English football. For the next three seasons they finished runners-up in the league, lost the 1970 FA Cup Final in a replay to Chelsea and won the 1972 FA Cup, failing narrowly to clinch the double. They did, however, add a second UEFA Cup to their haul in 1971 against Juventus and in 1974, Revie's last season, they finally cracked the League Championship again.

Brian Clough took over following Revie's departure for the England manager's job but was dismissed barely seven weeks into his tenure. Leeds did reach the European Cup final in 1975 but were beaten by Bayern Munich and against a backdrop of hooliganism and lack of success the next decade was one of decline, the ultimate blow being relegation in 1982. However, in 1988, Howard Wilkinson took over as manager, bought new players and regained first division status in 1990 before beating Manchester United to the championship in 1992.

Elland Road's emergence as a stadium of international standard was confirmed last June when it hosted England's first home game away from Wembley since 1966. The Umbro Cup game between England and Sweden ended in a dramatic 3-3 draw with England scoring twice in the last two minutes to the relief of the 32,000 crowd. Elland Road will be playing host to four of the best teams in Europe each bristling with international stars although what sort of good-humoured reception former Leeds United favourite, Eric Cantona, will get is hard to say.

The city is aiming to stage an ambitious range of events before and during the finals. More Than A Game, an interactive exhibition of football culture which explores and celebrates the fans' perspective, is planned for the summer. A month-long street music festival will run throughout June in Leeds City Centre and the spectacle will feature entertainers and performers from England as well as the four countries playing at Leeds; Spain, France, Bulgaria and Romania. The annual Lord Mayor's Parade will include floats designed to celebrate the city hosting the three games during the European Championship.

LIVERPOOL

Stadium: Anfield
Host club: Liverpool
Opened: 1892
Capacity: 41,000 for European Championship
Record: 61,905 v Wolves (1952)

MATCH SCHEDULE

Group C: Italy v Russia 11 June 4.30 pm
Czech Republic v Italy 14 June 7.30 pm
Russia v Czech Republic 19 June 7.30 pm
Quarter-final: 22 June 6.30 pm

Anfield was originally the home of Everton whose headquarters it was between 1892 and 1894. But after a dispute between club members, the majority left to create a new club and ground less than a mile away. So Goodison Park came into being while the remaining members stayed at Anfield and adopted a new name, Liverpool.

Liverpool's phenomenal record in the modern era began with the arrival of the messiah-like figure of Bill Shankly in December 1959. The club had won two league championships in the first decade of the century and two more in the early twenties but the 1950s witnessed the unthinkable: relegation.

Shankly took over a faded Liverpool side and exuding enthusaism he quickly established the roots of greatness. In two-and-a-half years he transformed the side and won them promotion from the second division. In 1964, Liverpool secured the league championship, a year later they won the FA Cup and the following year they won the league again. By the early seventies, Shankly had built an inspirational side and signed some the club's greatest servants such as Kevin Keegan, Emlyn Hughes, John Toshack and Ray Clemence and the trophies continued to accumulate.

Shankly had an eye for youthful talent and managerial expertise and his resignation was greeted with surprise and dismay by the Liverpool faithful. But the great measure of his influence has been the success the club has enjoyed since. Liverpool's secret for success has always been continuity and Shankly was succeeded by two of his former assistant coaches, the late Bob Paisley and Joe Fagin. Under Paisley, Liverpool achieved even greater success winning six championships, three European Cups and one UEFA Cup in nine years – making himself the most successful manager in British football history.

Young players tutored in the "Liverpool way" were drafted in to replace fading heroes so the generation of Hughes and Keegan gave way to the likes of Alan Hansen, Kenny Dalglish and Ian Rush. Dalglish himself became manager and led the club to achieve the league and cup double in 1986 just one year after the disaster at Heysel.

However, in 1989, the whole of Liverpool fell silent when 95 supporters were killed and almost 200 injured at Hillsborough before an FA Cup semi-final against Nottingham Forest. The disaster led to the dismantling of security fences and to the requirements of all-seater stadiums but the tragedy hit Liverpool hard. Even the ground's best-know feature, the Kop, for so long a mass of singing, chanting supporters, fell silent – the silence every bit as powerful as the roar which Shankley had believed was worth a goal a game.

Built in 1906 the Kop, named in honour of the famous hill Spion Kop where many local soldiers died in the Boer War, grew to become a powerful symbol of Liverpool's success and could accommodate 26,000 fans. As an all-seater stand, it has lost some of its magic but the Anfield is now one of the finest in Europe. Surprisingly, it has only staged several FA Cup semi-finals and internationals although it was the venue for the final place play-off between Holland and the Republic of Ireland.

Liverpool itself will be hosting a wide range of events during the championships including a spectacular river festival. Regattas, maritime displays and visits by famous ships are also planned to celebrate Liverpool's sea-faring history.

Musical events include an open air concert by the Royal Liverpool Philharmonic Orchestra, the Mathew Street festival, in memory of the Beatles, an African Oye festival featuring African and South American music as well as a series of pop concerts.

LONDON
Stadium: Wembley
Opened: 1923
Capacity: 76,000 for European Championship
Opening ceremony: 8 June 1.30 pm

MATCH SCHEDULE
Group A: England v Switzerland 8 June 3.00 pm
Scotland v England 15 June 3.00 pm
Holland v England 18 June 7.30 pm
Quarter-final: 22 June 3.00 pm
Semi-final: 26 June 7.30 pm
Final: 30 June 7.00 pm

There are more glamorous settings, bigger and better stadiums but despite its failings, Wembley, with its famous twin towers, is the home of English football and revered by fans and players throughout the world.

The stadium was built in the early 1920s to serve as the centre-piece for the British Empire Exhibition of 1924. The Wembley legend started from the very first game – the white horse FA Cup final between West Ham United and Bolton Wanderers in 1923. An estimated 200,000 people crammed into the stadium causing the game to be delayed by forty minutes as they spilled onto the pitch. The match went ahead, thanks in part to the efforts of a famous white police horse called Billie and his rider PC Scorey, and Bolton went on to win 2-0. The stadium has hosted the FA Cup final ever since.

As the venue of legends, Wembley stadium has hosted a variety of other sporting events. In 1948, it staged the Olympic Games, the rugby league stages its Challenge Cup finals and internationals there and regular American Football matches are played there. Indeed, the stadium became home to London's own grid iron team, the London Monarchs.

But football is the reason for the stadium's fame around the world and football has been the cause of the greatest moments in Wembley's history. In addition to the 'White Horse Cup Final', there was the 'Matthews Cup Final' of 1953, when Stanley Matthews orchestrated a 4-3 win for Blackpool over Bolton Wanderers; the highly emotional European Cup Final of 1968, when Sir Matt Busby's Manchester United beat Benfica 4-1 to become the first English club to be crowned European Champions, 10 years after the Munich air crash; the 1978 European Cup Final, when Liverpool won the title for the second year in succession, beating FC Brugge 1-0.

But the crowning glory, the greatest moment in English football history, was indisputably on 30 July, 1966, when Bobby Moore was handed the Jules Rimet Trophy by HM The Queen which meant that England were the world champions.

England played every game of the 1966 World Cup at Wembley and the psychological boost provided by this awe-inspiring stadium was probably worth a goal start every time. In those days the capacity was 100,000, a nice, round figure that you'd see year after year next to the Cup Final result, a magical figure that no other stadium in the country could match.

In the late eighties, the stadium was developed and the terraces began to disappear as seating was installed throughout and the capacity was necessarily reduced. Since these changes, the stadium has hosted two major international finals. The 1993 Cup Winners Cup Final drew only 37,393 supporters from Parma and Antwerp, but the European Cup Final the previous year had seen the stadium brought to life by 74,000 fans from Sampdoria and Barcelona, a foretaste of what can be expected from the European Championship. This summer the stadium will also relive the experience of hosting the Tartan Army, last seen at Wembley in 1988 when Peter Beardsley scored the only goal of the game.

MANCHESTER
Stadium: Old Trafford
Host club: Manchester United
Capacity: 43,000 for European Championship
Record: 76,962 v Arsenal (1920)

MATCH SCHEDULE
Group C: Germany v Czech Republic 9 June 5.00 pm
Russia v Germany 16 June 3.00 pm
Italy v Germany 19 June 7.30 pm
Quarter-final: 23 June 3.00 pm
Semi-final: 26 June 5.00 pm

Manchester United will unveil their new-look stadium for the European Championship. The £28 million development of the North Stand will be officially opened prior to the finals and the stadium, which has been virtually rebuilt in the past thirty years, will boast a 43,000 capacity for the finals with the potential, when it is completely finished, for Old Trafford to boast a capacity of 55,300.

The North Stand has replaced the original cantilever stand which included British football's first private boxes. Old Trafford's Stretford End was famous throughout the football world as the place where United's most fervent supporters would congregate. Originally an open terrace, it was covered in 1959 and then demolished in 1992 to make way for a new two-tier all-seater West Stand.

Old Trafford has, for many years, been regarded as the premier club stadium in England. That Manchester United can boast such riches is down to the vision and leadership of one man, the late Sir Matt Busby.

Sir Matt was a Scottish international wing-half who played before the Second World War for Liverpool and Manchester City. He took over as manager of United in 1945 when air-raid damage had reduced the stadium to near ruin. Such was his gift for management that, within three years, he had created the first of three memorable teams.

Busby assembled a brilliant attacking side under the captaincy of Johnny Carey to win the FA Cup in 1948 and from 1947 to 1949 they finished runners-up in the championship before finally lifting it in 1952. this signalled the end of Busby's first great side and in the early fifties he introduced a crop of talented youngsters to the first team and the legend of the Busby Babes was born.

Built around the mighty figure of Duncan Edwards, the Babes won the league championship in 1956 and 1957. United became the first English club to play in Europe in the 1956-57 season despite efforts by the football establishement to prevent them from doing so. They ignored the ban and reached the semi-finals of the European Cup before losing to eventual winners Real Madrid. They reached the same stage of the competition the following year, losing to Milan with a makeshift side hastily pulled together in the wake of the Munich air disaster in which eight players including Roger Byrne and Duncan Edwards were killed.

After the Munich air crash, Busby was forced to build again, forever in pursuit of the European Cup. His third great side, armed with the dazzling trinity of Charlton, Best and Law, won the championship twice, finished runners-up twice, won the FA Cup once and, in 1968, made the European dream a reality when they became the first English team to win the European Cup when they beat Benfica at Wembley.

Thereafter, United have experienced mixed fortunes but none who directly succeeded Busby could emulate his achievements. Tommy Docherty and Ron Atkinson created attractive teams but it wasn't until United's recent success under Alex Ferguson (two league championships, two FA Cups, one League Cup and one Cup Winners Cup) that the team has succeeded and entertained in the spirit loved by Busby and United's supporters.

This spirit and love of the game will be reflected in Manchester's staging of its European Championship games. It is putting together a month-long series of events to entertain football fans, visitors to the city and local residents alike. Under the banner of SoccerCity '96, a host of celebrations will take place all around the city centre – in clubs, galleries, cinemas, historic sites and the streets themselves. The opening event will coincide with the Lord Mayor's Parade where musicians and entertainers will add to the carnival atmosphere.

Many of the proposed events will be free. Theatres will stage plays of a football-related nature, a festival of football films will be shown at cinemas, local football tournaments will be organised as well as chat show evenings with football celebrities. The celebrations will end with a grand finale at the Castlefield Outdoor Events Arena.

NEWCASTLE
Stadium: St James' Park
Host club: Newcastle United
Opened: 1892
Capacity: 35,000 for European Championship
Record: 68,386 v Chelsea (1930)

MATCH SCHEDULE
Group B: Romania v France 10 June 7.30 pm
Bulgaria v Romania 13 June 4.30 pm
France v Bulgaria 18 June 4.30 pm

When Kevin Keegan was appointed manager of Newcastle United in February 1992 the club was facing relegation to Division 2. In just four years he has affected a dramatic turnaround in the club's fortunes. His threatened walk-out shortly after being appointed prompted the board to invest in a building programme that has taken Newcastle United to the very top. And as quickly as the team has blossomed, the ground has been transformed from a run-of-the-mill stadium into an impressive, modern arena almost overnight. Demand for tickets now outstrips demand by some 20,000.

Sir John Hall, the club chairman, now enjoys a stadium which is second to none in this country and against all this, Hall has instigated the creation of a sporting superstructure for the region, Newcastle United Sporting Club, which has incorporated rugby union, ice hockey and even the sponsorship of a GT car into the club's portfolio.

The club has come a long way since Newcastle West End joined Newcastle East End in 1892 to become Newcastle United and moved to Newcastle's Town Moor – to the ground which became St James' Park.

St James' Park received a new West Stand in 1906, concrete terracing in 1948 and a new East Stand in 1973. It was the first ground to be fitted with floodlights, in 1953, but by the 1990s the place had fallen behind other modern sports stadia.

The arrival of Sir John Hall, a new board and new money created the right conditions to develop the stadium into a football theatre for the next century. Work began in earnest and the first new construction, the Sir John Hall Stand, was opened in August 1993, with the

Exhibition Stand completed a year later. The Gallowgate and Leazes Ends were seated and a roof put on the whole thing, giving the ground a wonderful enclosed atmosphere.

Newcastle, it seems, are ending the 20th Century as they begun it, their ascendancy being long overdue for a city with such fervent footballing passions and such a rich source of players. The club's strongest era was the early part of the century, before World War I, when they won the league championship three times and the FA Cup once. Their next period of consistent success came in the fifties, when the prolific Jackie Milburn fired them to three FA Cups in 1951, 1952 and 1955, although they never threatened the league title again after their fourth championship in 1927. They did, however, qualify for the UEFA Cup in 1968 and won it at the first attempt.

What Keegan and Sir John Hall recognised was the power that lay in the club's fanatical following. Now that they have created a team and a stadium worthy of that support.

NOTTINGHAM
Stadium: City Ground
Host club: Nottingham Forest
Opened: 1898
Capacity: 30,500 for European Championship
Record: 49,946 v Manchester United (1967)

MATCH SCHEDULE
Group D: Turkey v Croatia 11 June 7.30 pm
Portugal v Turkey 14 June 4.30 pm
Croatia v Portugal 19 June 4.30 pm

The smallest of the championship venues, the City Ground has undergone major transformation in recent years and it is now one of the best appointed stadiums and will have an all-seater capacity of 30,500 for the finals.

The City Ground hosted its first international for 86 years last June when Japan played Sweden in the Umbro Cup but the attendance of only 5,591 was disappointing. The opportunity to see two of the dark horses of the European Championship finals, Portugal and Croatia, is a considerably more attractive proposition.

Nottingham Forest is one of the oldest clubs in the world. It was founded in 1865 under the name of the Forest Football Club and played at six different venues, including nearby Trent Bridge Cricket Ground, before moving to the City Ground in 1898. That year, Forest won their first major honours, the FA Cup, but, aside from a couple of Division 2 championships, they would have to wait until 1959 to repeat that FA Cup triumph.

In 1967, Forest came close to the league and cup double, finishing as runners-up and semi-finalists respectively. They were an attractive side but a decline in fortunes was imminent. The ill-judged purchase of the once-great Scottish international, Jim Baxter, and a fire which destroyed the City Ground's main stand were followed by the sale of several star players and Forest were relegated in 1972.

Three years later, along came a certain gentleman called Brian Clough. Working closely with his assistant Peter Taylor, he transformed a bunch of also-rans into a team which secured promotion to the first division in 1975, and won the league championship and League Cup in 1978. And it didn't stop there. Cloughie led his band of merry men, which included such influential players as John Robertson, Tony Woodcock and John McGovern, to win the European Cup in 1979 at the first attempt and successfully defended their title the following year. They had also retained the League Cup in 1979.

In their first five years at the City Ground, the Clough/Taylor partnership brought Nottingham Forest promotion, one League Championship, two European Cups, two League Cups, one Charity Shield, one European Super Cup and one Anglo-Scottish Cup.

During their heyday in the late seventies the all-seater executive stand was built opposite the Main Stand, with a capacity of almost 10,000 spectators. In the nineties, the unenclosed Bridgeford End terrace, which held around 13,000, was rebuilt as a two-tier, all-seater stand and now the Trent End, which held the Forest faithful, has been rebuilt in similar fashion. Both ends now hold over 7,000 fans.

Nottingham itself is an historic city, best known perhaps for its links with the legends of Robin Hood. Nottingham's celebrations will kick off with a spectacular launch event on 7 June in the Old Market Square which will also be the site for a two-week Euro fringe festival featuring music, street entertainment, food and crafts throughout the period the games are on.

A five-day medieval festival from 8 to 12 June will be centred around Nottingham Castle and there will also be a riverside extravaganza along the River Trent and Embankment on match days featuring boat races between fans to create a festive feeling.

SHEFFIELD
Stadium: Hillsborough
Host club: Sheffield Wednesday
Opened: 1899
Capacity: 40,000 for European Championship
Record: 72,841 v Manchester City (1934)

MATCH SCHEDULE
Group D: Denmark v Portugal 9 June 7.30 pm
Croatia v Denmark 16 June 6.00 pm
Turkey v Denmark 19 June 4.30 pm

Sheffield Wednesday, the fifth oldest club in the football league, took up residence at Hillsborough in 1899. The ground was originally named Owlerton, from which the club took its nickname, The Owls, but was renamed Hillsborough in 1912.

The Owls garnered a succession of honours around the turn of the century with first division championships in 1903 and 1904 and FA Cup triumphs in 1896 and 1907. They had to wait another 22 years for their next league title in 1929 but followed it promptly by retaining it the following year.

It is tradition rather than glory that has maintained Sheffield Wednesday's stature in English football. Sheffield was one of the creative centres of early association football and Wednesday were one of the first clubs, formed in 1867 by the Wednesday Cricket Club – so named because the founders were a group of local craftsmen whose weekly half-day was on a Wednesday.

Hillsborough's capacity has made it one of the first-choice venues for FA Cup semi-finals, but it was the semi-final of 1989 between Liverpool and Nottingham Forest which was to bring about the most radical change in English stadia ever.

The events of the Hillsborough disaster are well documented and the conclusion drawn was that it could have happened anywhere. It was decided that standing accommodation was unsafe and should be replaced with seating. Other safety measures were enforced and Sheffield Wednesday, not surprisingly, were quick to react. The Leppings Lane End, at which the fatal crush occurred, was redeveloped into an all-seater stand. The upper tier had been seated already but now the seating of the terrace below reduced the capacity of the whole end. The home supporters' end, as at Liverpool known as the Spion Kop, was also turned into an all-seater stand.

The stadium had undergone a major transformation in recent years with the completion of the new South Stand enabling the ground's capacity to be increased to 40,000.

Sheffield has a unique place in the history of football and is planning a major cultural festival to support the championships. With thousands of fans arriving from Portugal, Denmark, Turkey and Croatia the city is aiming to develop cultural links with each of the visiting teams' countries.

The principal events of the "Sheffield Play at Home" programme will start on 8 June with a carnival parade through the city featuring bands, clowns and jugglers and the city centre will be treated to a day packed with entertainment. On 9 June, Cafe Continental will provide a dynamic programme of world music which will reflect the interests and cultures of the four teams. The celebrations move to Sheffield's recently renovated Canal Basin, the Victoria Quays, for a Jazz festival on 15/16 June and the programme concludes with a final day of streeet entertainment and an evening of fire juggling and a fireworks display.

THE
EUROPEAN CHAMPIONSHIP
HISTORY

Surprisingly, considering that there were so many opportunities for international football games, Europe was the last continent to develop a championship for its member countries. This was due in part to strong regional tournaments, such as the British International Championship (better known as the home internationals) between England, Scotland, Wales and Ireland (Northern Ireland after 1921); the International Cup, which brought together Italy, Austria, Czechoslovakia and Hungary, as well as Switzerland and Yugoslavia; and a number of other tournaments, such as the Scandinavian Championship, Balkan Cup and Baltic Cup.

Just as we have a Frenchman, Jules Rimet, to thank for the World Cup, we are indebted to his fellow countryman Henri Delaunay, the French football administrator and first general secretary of UEFA, for persevering with his idea for a unifying European tournament. With the creation of UEFA in 1954, the realization of Delaunay's dream came a step closer, but sadly he died in 1955, a year before his vision was accepted by UEFA and FIFA and named the European Nations Cup, to be contested every four years, between the World Cup tournaments.

1960 Like the World Cup three decades earlier, the European Championship had somewhat humble beginnings. The first rounds of the inaugural tournament began in 1958, but only seventeen teams entered. Neither West Germany nor Italy took part, and of the home countries of Great Britain, only the Republic of Ireland entered, losing to Czechoslovakia in a two-leg preliminary tie. England's sole contribution to the competition was Arthur Ellis, who refereed the final in Paris.

The European Nations Cup, a title the competition was to retain until 1966, pitted the remaining sixteen teams on a home-and-away knock-out basis, similar to that of the European club competitions, switching to sudden death for the semi-final and final, which were played in one host country chosen from one of the four semi-finalists.

The Soviet Union, with such notable players as Netto, Ivanov, Simonian and the brilliant goalkeeper Yashin, had qualified for their first-ever World Cup finals in 1958, eliminating England in the group stage before losing to Sweden in the quarter-finals. For the European Nations Cup, the side was further strengthened by the addition of Metreveli and Ponedelnik. Having beaten Hungary, no longer the sublime force of the early 1950s, in the opening round, the Soviet Union were given a walkover in the quarter-finals when General Franco's Spain refused to play them on political grounds.

France had finished third in the 1958 World Cup after losing a memorable semi-final 5-2 to eventual winners Brazil. Fontaine and Kopa had proved an irresistible strike force in Sweden and continued their prolific scoring in the opening round as France put seven past Greece, effectively deciding the outcome over the first leg.

In the quarter-finals, France beat Austria 5-2 at home and 4-2 away, while Czechoslovakia won both legs against Romania. Yugoslavia's route was more adventurous. After a steady win against Bulgaria in the opening round, they beat Portugal 5-1 in Belgrade following a 2-1 defeat in Lisbon.

Fittingly, France was chosen as the host venue for the final series but for them the competition was to end in disappointment. The French lost their inspirational goalscorer, Fontaine, for the semi-final against Yugoslavia, but with just fifteen minutes left they were leading comfortably by 4-2. However, with three goals in under five minutes, from Knez and Jerkovic (two), the Yugoslavs rallied round to beat their hosts 5-4 in a thrilling game of many fluctuations. In the other semi-final, the Soviet Union beat the emerging Czechs 3-0 in Marseilles, their agile, black-clad goalkeeper, Yashin, thwarting the opposition time and again.

The final in Paris was always going to be close. Yashin in the Soviet goal was once again in superb form, but Yugoslavia went ahead when Galic's shot was deflected into the net by Netto just before half-time. After the interval, the Soviet Union stepped up their game, Metreveli equalized ten minutes into the half and Ponedelnik secured the trophy with a goal in extra time.

PRELIMINARY ROUND

Republic of Ireland	2	–	0	Czechoslovakia
Czechoslovakia	4	–	0	Republic of Ireland

FIRST ROUND

Soviet Union	3	–	1	Hungary
Hungary	0	–	1	Soviet Union
Poland	2	–	4	Spain
Spain	3	–	0	Poland
France	7	–	1	Greece
Greece	1	–	1	France
Romania	3	–	0	Turkey
Turkey	2	–	0	Romania
Norway	0	–	1	Austria
Austria	5	–	2	Norway
Yugoslavia	2	–	0	Bulgaria
Bulgaria	1	–	1	Yugoslavia
Denmark	2	–	2	Czechoslovakia
Czechoslovakia	5	–	1	Denmark
Portugal	3	–	2	East Germany
East Germany	0	–	2	Portugal

QUARTER-FINALS

Soviet Union v Spain. Soviet Union walked over as
Spain withdrew

Romania	0	– 2	Czechoslovakia
Czechoslovakia	3	– 0	Romania
France	5	– 2	Austria
Austria	2	– 4	France
Portugal	2	– 1	Yugoslavia
Yugoslavia	5	– 1	Portugal

SEMI-FINALS

Soviet Union	3	– 0	Czechoslovakia
Yugoslavia	5	– 4	France

THIRD-PLACE PLAY-OFF

Czechoslovakia	2	– 0	France

FINAL Parc de Princes, Paris att: 18,000 10 July 1964

Soviet Union	2	– 1	Yugoslavia (after extra time)

1964

The second tournament was organized on the same two-leg, knock-out basis as the inaugural series, and with twenty-nine of the thirty-three eligible countries agreeing to compete – among them England, Wales and Northern Ireland – the tournament was poised to attract a lot more interest than the first. West Germany and Scotland were two notable absentees.

Three teams, Austria, Luxembourg and the Soviet Union, were given byes to balance the second-round number to sixteen, and of the remaining thirteen ties, Greece refused to play Albania as the two countries had been in a state of uneasy truce for many years. UEFA awarded the tie to Albania.

England's entry marked the start, albeit inauspiciously, of Sir Alf Ramsey's twelve-year reign as manager. Handed the uninspiring foundation of a 1-1 draw at home to France on taking over from Walter Winterbottom, Ramsey went to France with a team which included a five-man forward line of Charlton, Connelly, Greaves, Smith and Tambling. Smith and Tambling did indeed score but England were already 3-0 down by that stage and the French eventually finished 5-2 winners. Rarely had England suffered such a heavy defeat, and although the French were hard to break down in defence and superior in attack, a series of errors by Springett, the England goalkeeper, contributed to the defeat. In only the third minute, the French winger, Wisnieski easily scored past the advancing 'keeper, Douis made it two thirty minutes later, and then Springett feebly pushed out Wisnieski's cross straight to Cossou, who rifled it into the empty net just before half-time for 3-0.

After the break, Greaves hit the post for England before Smith cut the deficit with a neat header. Tambling scored from a corner fifteen minutes from time, yet no sooner were England back in the match than their defence collapsed. Once again it was a shot from Wisnieski which did the damage. It rebounded from Springett to Cossou, who laid it back for Wisnieski to score. Minutes later, Cossou lobbed Springett for his second and France's fifth.

Ramsey had hoped to use a good run in the tournament as preparation for the 1966 World Cup, but now he had to return to face public and media criticism befoe he could look ahead to creating a World Cup-winning team.

Wales also went out in the first round, to a revived Hungarian team, but Northern Ireland, still buoyant after the 1958 World Cup, registered with two brilliant 2-0 victories over Poland to reach the second round, where they joined the Republic of Ireland, who had beaten Iceland 5-3 on aggregate.

World Cup runners-up Czechoslovakia, one of the favourites to win the tournament, were beaten by the East Germans, who won their home tie 2-1 and then resolutely defended their advantage in Prague.

Of the remaining ties, Spain, Holland, Denmark, Yugoslavia and Italy qualified comfortably; Sweden were made to struggle by Scandinavian neighbours Norway, and in the tightest tie of all Bulgaria beat Portugal 1-0 in a play-off after both teams had won their respective home legs by 3-1.

The draw for the second round paired Northern Ireland, now without their influential captain, Blanchflower, who had retired from international football, with Spain. Northern Ireland played extremely well to earn a deserved draw in Spain but lost the home leg in Belfast 1-0.

The most eagerly awaited tie of the round was between the Soviet Union and Italy. The first leg took place on 13 October 1963 in Moscow, and attracted 102,400 spectators. They witnessed a frenetic first half. Italian striker Sormani had to leave the field with a head injury after just twelve minutes and ten minutes later Ponedelnik put the Soviet Union one up. Italy, already down to ten men, lost another player when Pascutti was sent off for head-butting Dubinski. Sormani returned to the field, but Chislenko made it 2-0 just before half-time and the Soviet Union held on to their lead comfortably for the remainder of the game.

The following month, the great Soviet goalkeeper Yashin was recalled for the return leg in Rome for what was expected to be an Italian onslaught. However, an early goal by Gusarov eased the Soviets' task, and despite Italy's desperate assault on Yashin's goal, the 'keeper dealt with everything they could throw at him – even a fifty-seventh-minute penalty from Mazzola. Italy did equalize in the final minute, but by then it was far too late.

The most remarkable performance of the tournament belonged to Luxembourg in their match against Holland. Forsaking home advantage, Luxembourg elected to play both their games away, drawing 1-1 in Amsterdam and winning their 'home' leg in Rotterdam by 2-1. Dimmer scored both goals in the second leg and Schmitt, in the Luxembourg goal, produced a string of fine saves, despite finishing the game with a dislocated shoulder.

Denmark easily disposed of Albania and Sweden, France, Hungary and the Republic of Ireland all won tough, close-fought ties against Yugoslavia, Bulgaria, East Germany and Austria respectively.

In the latter stages of the tournament, Spain basked in the creative skills of Suarez, with Marcellino and Amancio giving the attack a cutting edge. In the quarter-finals they cruised past the Republic of Ireland by 7-1 on aggregate. Hungary also achieved a relatively comfortable passage past France, winning both legs.

Despite their heroics against Holland, Luxembourg were not expected to present much of a barrier to Denmark's progress to the semi-finals. All predictions were dismissed within the first minute as Pilot gave Luxembourg the lead. Madsen equalized twice for the Danes to end the half at 2-2 and then put Denmark ahead with a third. But Luxembourg weren't beaten yet: they levelled the game 3-3. In the return leg six days later, Luxembourg again took an early lead before Madsen equalized in the first half and then, once again, gave his country the lead with twenty minutes remaining. Minutes from time, Schmit brought Luxembourg back to 2-2 and a play-off in Amsterdam. It was Madsen (who else?) who scored for Denmark in the play-off, just before half-time, to finally put the tie beyond Luxembourg's powers of recovery.

In the fourth quarter-final, Sweden, who had already beaten the previous runners-up, Yugoslavia, now prepared to face the champions, the Soviet Union, in a compelling tie. The first leg, played in Stockholm in May 1964, ended in a 1-1 draw, Sweden's Hamrin equalizing Ivanov's early strike.

Before the start of the return leg in Moscow, Yashin was presented with the European Footballer of the Year trophy for 1963. He justified this honour with another superb display which kept the Swedish attack at bay. Ponedelnik put the Soviet Union ahead shortly before half-time with a rare foray into Swedish territory, and increased their advantage in the sixtieth minute before Hamrin pulled one back for Sweden. Voronin dashed any Swedish hopes of a recovery with a well-taken third.

Spain was chosen as the venue for the semi-finals. Barcelona saw the Soviet Union beat Denmark with goals from Voronin, Ponedelnik and Ivanov to seal their second consecutive appearance in the Nations Cup final. Spain had a tougher game against Hungary in Madrid before Amancio scored the decisive goal in extra time for a 2-1 victory.

The third-place match was played the day before the final and this too went into extra time, Bertelsen's having equalized for Denmark in the eighty-first minute after Bene had put Hungary ahead in the eleventh. Two goals for Novak – one a penalty, the second a thunderous free kick, clinched third place for Hungary, but the Danes had played with the sort of spirit which would reap rewards in 1984 and most memorably, 1992.

The final between Spain and the Soviet Union was played in front of General Franco and 105,000 others in the Bernabeu Stadium in Madrid. The Spanish took the lead after only six minutes when Suarez intercepted Ivanov's pass from defence and provided Pereda with a simple opportunity. Within minutes the home crowd were groaning in dismay as the Spanish goalkeeper, Iribar, allowed Khusainov's weak shot to squirm into the net. With seven minutes remaining Marcellino won the match for Spain in typical style, flinging himself low to head past Yashin. Spain might have lacked the creativity and skill of the great Real Madrid sides which had dominated the European Cup, but they deserved their victory nonetheless.

FIRST ROUND

Spain	6	– 0	Romania
Romania	3	– 1	Spain
Poland	0	– 2	Northern Ireland
Northern Ireland	2	– 0	Poland
Republic of Ireland	4	– 2	Iceland
Iceland	1	– 1	Republic of Ireland
Bulgaria	3	– 1	Portugal
Portugal	3	– 1	Bulgaria
Bulgaria	1	– 0	Portugal (Rome)
England	1	– 1	France
France	5	– 2	England
East Germany	2	– 1	Czechoslovakia
Czechoslovakia	1	– 1	East Germany
Hungary	3	– 1	Wales
Wales	1	– 1	Hungary
Denmark	6	– 1	Malta

Malta   1 – 3   Denmark
Albania v Greece (Albanian walkover as Greece withdrew)
Holland   3 – 1   Switzerland
Switzerland   1 – 1   Holland
Norway   0 – 2   Sweden
Sweden   1 – 1   Norway
Yugoslavia   3 – 2   Belgium
Belgium   0 – 1   Yugoslavia
Italy   6 – 0   Turkey
Turkey   0 – 1   Italy
Austria bye
Luxembourg bye
Soviet Union bye

SECOND ROUND

Spain   1 – 1   Northern Ireland
Northern Ireland   0 – 1   Spain
Austria   0 – 0   Republic of Ireland
Republic of Ireland   3 – 2   Austria
Bulgaria   1 – 0   France
France   3 – 1   Bulgaria
East Germany   1 – 2   Hungary
Hungary   3 – 3   East Germany
Denmark   4 – 0   Albania
Albania   1 – 0   Denmark
Holland   1 – 1   Luxembourg
Luxembourg   2 – 1   Holland
Yugoslavia   0 – 0   Sweden
Sweden   3 – 2   Yugoslavia
Soviet Union   2 – 0   Italy
Italy   1 – 1   Soviet Union

QUARTER FINALS

Spain	5	–	1	Republic of Ireland
Republic of Ireland	0	–	2	Spain
France	1	–	3	Hungary
Hungary	2	–	1	France
Luxembourg	3	–	3	Denmark
Denmark	2	–	2	Luxembourg
Denmark	1	–	0	Luxembourg (Amsterdam)
Sweden	1	–	1	Soviet Union
Soviet Union	3	–	1	Sweden

SEMI-FINALS

Spain	2	–	1	Hungary
Soviet Union	3	–	0	Denmark

THIRD-PLACE PLAY-OFF

Hungary	3	–	1	Denmark

FINAL Bernabeu Stadium, Madrid att: 105,000 21 June 1964

Spain	2	–	1	Soviet Union

1968 The tournament was renamed the European Championship for the third series and, as West Germany and Scotland now agreed to take part, qualifying groups were introduced to replace the previous first- and second-round two-leg knock-out system. The thirty-one entrants were split into eight groups with a seeded team, also a first, in each. The group winners would progress to the quarter-finals, to be played on a home-and-away knock-out basis as before to decide the four semi-finalists. The host nation for the final stages would again be chosen from the last four.

Since suffering the disappointment of failing to qualify for the previous tournament, Alf Ramsey's wingless wonders had fulfilled his daring prophecy that England would win the 1966 World Cup. Now they were the seeded team in Group Eight which included Scotland, Northern Ireland and Wales. In 1965, it had been agreed that the home internationals of seasons 1966-67 and 1967-68 should be used as an eliminating competition for the European Championship. The group soon developed into a race between England and Scotland.

All the ingredients for a classic game were in place for their first meeting. England, the world champions, were unbeaten in nineteen successive internationals and playing at Wembley, where they had achieved their memorable triumph just nine months previously. Scotland had failed to reach the World Cup finals, despite possessing a team which would have been a serious contender, and had a score to settle.

Bobby Charlton later reflected that if he had been asked who would be the first team to beat England after the World Cup he would always have said the Scots. And so it proved. For almost the entire match the Scots dictated proceedings with little regard for the reputation of the world champions. So many Scottish fans had travelled south that the game seemed almost like a home fixture for the Scots. To their delight, Law put the visitors ahead in the first half, but they had to wait until twelve minutes from time for Scotland's second goal, from the Celtic striker Lennox. Jack Charlton pulled one back for England before McCalliog beat Banks to make it 3-1. Even then Hurst kept the issue in doubt with another header, but the score remained at 3-2.

Scotland were now favourites to qualify from Group Eight, but then they were defeated in Belfast, where Best, at his mercurial peak, inspired the Irish to a 1-0 victory. The Scots therefore needed to repeat their win over England in the return leg at Hampden Park, but even the huge crowd of 134,000 failed to lift the home team to the win they so desperately wanted. England secured qualification with a solid 1-1 draw.

The reigning European champions, Spain, were expected to qualify easily from Group One but they were held to 0-0 away draws against Turkey and the Republic of Ireland. Spain put matters right in the return legs, but then suffered a further setback against Czechoslovakia when the Spanish goalkeeper, Iribar, totally mistimed his dive at Horvath's speculative shot. Three weeks later the two countries met again in Madrid, where a much-improved Spanish side won 2-1 with goals from Pirri and Garate.

Spain, their games completed, led the group by two points, but Czechoslovakia were only two points behind them with two games remaining and looked sure to qualify. They duly picked up their first point away to Turkey and fielded a full-strength side for their home game against the Republic of Ireland who were forced, through injuries, to select inexperienced players from the League's lower divisions. Fifteen minutes into the second half, Dempsey scored an own goal, but the Czechs' lead was short-lived. Treacy headed home to level matters, and then, with just four minutes remaining, created an opening for O'Connor to score a winner which was met with incredulity all over Europe and considerable thanks in Spain.

Portugal were firm favourites to win Group Two. They had finished third in the 1966 World Cup, were unbeaten at home since May 1964 and had one of the greatest players ever, Eusebio da Silva Ferreira. But their opening game at home to Sweden was to produce something of a shock and cost them dear. Despite taking the lead through Graca, the Portuguese were powerless to stop Danielsson's 30-yard screamer of an equalizer just before half-time and were stunned by Danielsson again late in the game.

Sweden's challenge faltered and Portugal returned to their winning ways, but it was Bulgaria who sealed a quarter-final place, and by a four-point margin, with a 1-0 victory over Portugal in Sofia followed by a 0-0 draw in Lisbon.

Group Three predictably went to the Soviet Union, who also

topped it by four clear points. The only serious obstacle to their progress was provided by Austria, who battled bravely in Moscow only to lose 4-3 and won the return leg in Vienna through Grausam's strike.

Word Cup finalists West Germany made their first appearance in the European Championship in a three-team group with Yugoslavia and Albania, and so looked set for an easy debut. In their first game, the Germans beat Albania 6-0 but they lost narrowly to Yugoslavia in Belgrade. In the return leg goals by Lohr, Müller and Seeler restored West Germany's position, and Yugoslavia beat Albania for a second time. It seemed unthinkable that the Germans would not do so as well.

But the Albanians, undoubtedly still smarting from their 6-0 humiliation, defended stoutly, refusing to allow the Germans the time and space they wanted. Despite constant pressure, West Germany couldn't break through and were out of their first championship in the preliminary stages.

In Group Five, the Hungarians had created another supremely gifted side which was attracting favourable comparisons to the Magical Magyars of the 1950s. With nine points from their first five games, including a brilliant performance in beating East Germany 3-1, they qualified comfortably.

Following their humiliation in the 1966 World Cup finals, Italy had returned home to a bombardment of rotten vegetables from disappointed fans. Keen to rid themselves of this memory, they put together the best series of results of all the qualifiers and dropped only one point, in a 2-2 draw with Switzerland.

In the remaining group, Luxembourg were unable to repeat their heroics of the previous tournament and took up their more customary position propping up the table. However, France, Belgium and Poland were evenly matched and all won their home legs in the early stages. Poland seemed to lose their chance when they were beaten at home by France, but the following month they won 4-2 away to Belgium to restore their hopes. France then drew at home to Belgium, which left them equal on points with Poland, who had finished their programme. Belgium predictably beat Luxembourg to join the others on seven points. It was France who took the group by two points by beating Luxembourg, although it was a close game.

The quarter-finals brought together the reigning world champions, England, and European champions Spain. The first leg was played at Wembley in April 1968, and although England created numerous scoring chances, the anxious crowd of 100,000 had to wait until five minutes from the end before Bobby Charlton put the home side ahead. Even then, Banks was called upon to make a spendid save from Grosso in the dying seconds. In Madrid, the English defence stood firm and goals by Peters and Hunter saw them comfortably through to their first semi-final.

Yugoslavia enjoyed a straightforward passage to the semis beating France 5-1 in Belgrade after drawing 1-1 in Marseilles.

Italy, who had qualified so convincingly from the group stages, lost the opening leg of their quarter-final against Bulgaria by 3-2 and were under considerable pressure to do better in the return leg in Naples, not least from their expectant fans. A fourteenth-minute strike from Prati calmed Italian fears and Domenghini put them 2-0 up in the second half, a position the Italians were never going to surrender. The Soviet Union also had it all to do in their home leg after losing 2-0 to Hungary in Budapest. They came through with a strong second-half performance to win 3-0.

Italy was chosen as the host country for the finals. The semi-finals drew them against the Soviet Union and England against Yugoslavia. In the first game, neither Italy nor the Soviet Union could break the stalemate in a game of poor quality but some excitement. Italy lost Rivera early on and missed his controlling influence. Shortly before half-time the Russians won six corners, but without their own star striker, Chislenko, they, too, struggled in front of goal. The second half remained goalless, and although the partisan crowd urged on their team the Russian defence were steadfast. Both teams looked tired in extra time but a late onslaught by the Italians nearly earned a vital goal when Domenghini's shot hit the post. Incredibly, the solution to the stalemate was not a penalty shoot-out but the toss of a coin which landed in favour of Italy, who thus progressed to their first European Championship final.

The second semi-final was a tough, uncompromising game in which Yugoslavia matched England's physical approach. By the tenth minute Osim, Yugoslavia's elegant midfielder, had been reduced to a limping passenger following a tackle by Hunter. What little creative football there was came from England. Charlton and Ball worked tirelessly but were often faced with a ten-man defence. As the game neared its end, England launched attack after attack in an attempt to settle the issue. Charlton shot just over the bar and into the side netting, while Moore, Newton and Hunter also tried to break the dead-lock. A swift counter-attack caught England's defence upfield and Petkovic curled a centre for Dzajic to chest down and hook into the net. England staged a tremendous last-minute rally but to no avail, and with seconds to go Mullery acquired the dubious distinction of being the first English player ever to be sent off in an international. The world champions were out.

Three days later, England faced the Soviet Union in Rome in the third-place play-off match and in the won the best game of the tournament 2-0 with a goal in each half from Bobby Charlton and Hurst. With the return of Stiles among the team changes, England played with a fresh gusto and their performance gave some consolation in a tournament they could have won. Their all-round teamwork had been excellent: what they lacked was a natural striker who could also conjure goals from nothing. Too much of this burden fell on Bobby Charlton.

The final was also played in Rome's Olympic Stadium later the same day. Fielding a virtually unchanged side, Yugoslavia dominated the first half. The home crowd had seldom seen their team's famed defence made to look so fragile, and it was surprising that Yugoslavia finished the first half only 1-0 ahead, by a goal from Dzajic in the fortieth minute. Zoff, in the Italian goal, kept his team in the game with a series of excellent second-half saves and in the eighty-first minute his efforts were rewarded when Italy drew level. Yugoslavia conceded a free kick 25 yards out and Domenghini's fierce drive flew into the net as the referee was still directing the Yugoslavian defensive wall to move further back. Despite protests from the defending side, the goal was allowed to stand and the match entered extra time. The Yugoslavs were too tired to regain control and a replay was arranged for two days later.

For the replay, Mazzola, de Sisti and Riva were brought back into the home side alongside Facchetti and Anastasi, and the Italians looked a stronger proposition. Yugoslavia again fielded virtually the same team, but this time Italy took command and their forwards were allowed space to play by a jaded team which had lost its physical challenge. Riva put the Italians ahead and Anastasi made it two on the half-hour with a powerful right-foot shot after which the game drifted into something of an anticlimax.

Italy thus became the second host nation to win the tournament, but it had been an uninspired championship and what sporadic moments of creativity there were had been overshadowed by cynical tactics.

QUALIFYING TOURNAMENT

GROUP ONE	P	W	D	L	F	A	Pts
Spain	6	3	2	1	6	2	8
Czechoslovakia	6	3	1	2	8	4	7
Republic of Ireland	6	2	1	3	5	8	5
Turkey	6	1	2	3	3	8	4

Republic of Ireland 0 Spain 0; Republic of Ireland 2 Turkey 1; Spain 2 Republic of Ireland 0; Turkey 0 Spain 0; Turkey 2 Republic of Ireland 1; Republic of Ireland 0 Czecholslovakia 2; Spain 2 Turkey 0; Czechoslovakia 3 Turkey 0; Czechoslovakia 1 Spain 0; Spain 2 Czechoslovakia 1; Turkey 0 Czechoslovakia 0; Czechoslovakia 1 Republic of Ireland 2

GROUP TWO	P	W	D	L	F	A	Pts
Bulgaria	6	4	2	0	10	2	10
Portugal	6	2	2	2	6	6	6
Sweden	6	2	1	3	9	12	5
Norway	6	1	1	4	9	14	3

Portugal 1 Sweden 2; Bulgaria 4 Norway 2; Sweden 1 Portugal 1; Norway 1 Portugal 2; Sweden 0 Bulgaria 2; Norway 0 Bulgaria 0; Norway 3 Sweden 1; Sweden 5 Norway 2; Bulgaria 3 Sweden 0; Portugal 2 Norway 1; Bulgaria 1 Portugal 0; Portugal 0 Bulgaria 0

GROUP THREE	P	W	D	L	F	A	Pts
Soviet Union	6	5	0	1	16	6	10
Greece	6	2	2	2	8	9	6
Austria	6	2	2	2	8	10	6
Finland	6	0	2	4	5	12	2

Finland 0 Austria 0; Greece 2 Finland 1; Finland 1 Greece 1; Soviet
Union 4 Austria 3; Soviet Union 4 Greece 0; Soviet Union 2 Finland 0;
Finland 2 Soviet Union 5; Austria 2 Finland 1; Greece 4 Austria 1;
Austria 1 Soviet Union 0; Greece 0 Soviet Union 1; Austria 1 Greece 1

GROUP FOUR	P	W	D	L	F	A	Pts
Yugoslavia	4	3	0	1	8	3	6
West Germany	4	2	1	1	9	2	5
Albania	4	0	1	3	0	12	1

West Germany 6 Albania 0; Yugoslavia 1 West Germany 0; Albania 0
Yugoslavia 2; West Germany 3 Yugoslavia 1; Yugoslavia 4 Albania 0;
Albania 0 West Germany 0

GROUP FIVE	P	W	D	L	F	A	Pts
Hungary	6	4	1	1	15	5	9
East Germany	6	3	1	2	10	10	7
Holland	6	2	1	3	11	11	5
Denmark	6	1	1	4	6	16	3

Holland 2 Hungary 2; Hungary 6 Denmark 0; Holland 2 Denmark 0;
East Germany 4 Holland 3; Hungary 2 Holland 1; Denmark 0 Hungary 2;
Denmark 1 East Germany 1; Holland 1 East Germany 0; Hungary 3
East Germany 1; Denmark 3 Holland 2; East Germany 3 Denmark 2;
East Germany 1 Hungary 0

GROUP SIX	P	W	D	L	F	A	Pts
Italy	6	5	1	0	17	3	11
Romania	6	3	0	3	18	14	6
Switzerland	6	2	1	3	17	13	5
Cyprus	6	1	0	5	3	25	2

Romania 4 Switzerland 2; Italy 3 Romania 1; Cyprus 1 Romania 5;
Cyprus 0 Italy 2; Romania 7 Cyprus 0; Switzerland 7 Romania 1; Italy 5
Cyprus 0; Switzerland 5 Cyprus 0; Switzerland 2 Italy 2; Italy 4
Switzerland 0; Cyprus 2 Switzerland 1; Romania 0 Italy 1

GROUP SEVEN	P	W	D	L	F	A	Pts
France	6	4	1	1	14	6	9
Belgium	6	3	1	2	14	9	7
Poland	6	3	1	2	13	9	7
Luxembourg	6	0	1	5	1	18	1

Poland 4 Luxembourg 0; France 2 Poland 1; Belgium 2 France 1;
Luxembourg 0 France 3; Luxembourg 0 Poland 0; Luxembourg 0
Belgium 5; Poland 3 Belgium 1; Poland 1 France 4; Belgium 2 Poland 4;
France 1 Belgium 1; Belgium 3 Luxembourg 0; France 3 Luxembourg 1

GROUP EIGHT	P	W	D	L	F	A	Pts
England	6	4	1	1	15	5	9
Scotland	6	3	2	1	10	8	8
Wales	6	1	2	3	6	12	4
Northern Ireland	6	1	1	4	2	8	3

Northern Ireland 0 England 2; Wales 1 Scotland 1; England 5 Wales 1;
Scotland 2 Northern Ireland 1; Northern Ireland 0 Wales 0; England 2
Scotland 3; Wales 0 England 3; Northern Ireland 0; England 2
Northern Ireland 0; Scotland 3 Wales 2; Scotland 1 England 1;
Wales 2 Northern Ireland 0

QUARTER-FINALS

Bulgaria	3	–	2	Italy
Italy	2	–	0	Bulgaria
Hungary	2	–	0	Soviet Union
Soviet Union	3	–	0	Hungary
England	1	–	0	Spain
Spain	1	–	2	England
France	1	–	1	Yugoslavia
Yugoslavia	5	–	1	France

SEMI-FINALS

Italy	0	-	0	Soviet Union (Italy won on toss of coin)
Yugoslavia	1	-	0	England

THIRD-PLACE PLAY-OFF

England	2	-	0	Soviet Union

FINAL Olympic Stadium, Rome att: 85,000 8 June 1968

Italy	1	-	1	Yugoslavia

REPLAY Olympic Stadium, Rome att: 85,000 10 June 1968

Italy	2	-	0	Yugoslavia

1972 Following the dour performances on display four years previously there was considerable optimism that the seventies would bring a new age of stylish and creative football. Brazil had made the game look a joy to play in winning the 1970 World Cup in glorious style and the onus was now on Europe to respond with a championship to match the South Americans' exploits and at the same time to erase the memories of the lacklustre 1968 tournament.

This was undoubtedly West Germany's tournament, and it marked the first stage of their development into a dominant force. The team epitomized the new age of total football. Beckenbauer demonstrated the art of the attacking sweeper with his brilliant ability to read the game; Netzer was the inspiration in midfield; Müller led the attack with an instinct for scoring goals. Indeed, the whole team showed exciting versatility.

Yet West Germany's exquisite talents were far from evident during their early qualifying Group Eight games against Albania and Turkey. A shock 1-1 draw at home to Turkey, saved by Müller's penalty, was followed by a slender 1-0 away win over Albania, again courtesy of a goal from Müller. After that, however, the Germans exerted their customary control over the group with impressive away wins against Turkey and Poland, who were also emerging as a major force in world football.

Group One brought Wales, Romania, Czechoslovakia and Finland together. The Czechs were favourites to qualify but their team was severely weakened when many of their World Cup stars were banned for alleged commercial activities. They could manage only a draw against Finland in Prague, and that dropped point was to prove vital. The banned players were reinstated, and although Czechoslovakia suffered only one defeat, 2-1 away to Romania, the damage had been done and it was Romania who went through on goal difference.

In Group Two, France once again found themselves in a three-way tussle for qualification, this time with Hungary and Bulgaria. The fortunes of each team swung wildly but it was Hungary who maintained the most consistent form to win the group.

Group Three looked a formality for England against Switzerland, Greece and Malta, but although they qualified with an unbeaten run, the favourites did not perform in the manner of potential champions.

Switzerland and England both made short work of Greece and Malta, and in the first meeting between the two leading teams, England were somewhat fortunate to come away from Basle with a 3-2 win, achieved through a Weibels' own goal when the scores were level at 2-2. England were also made to struggle in the return leg at Wembley, although the team had admittedly been weakened through club commitments. Odermatt put the Swiss ahead, but Summerbee's equalizer saved any embarrassment. England qualified safely with a 2-0 win in Greece.

Northern Ireland faced a tough prospect in Group Four, where they were to meet Spain, the Soviet Union and Cyprus, who went on to lose all six games. Northern Ireland held the two favourites to 1-1 draws at home but they had already lost any remote chance of qualification with a 3-0 defeat in Spain and a 1-0 reverse in the Soviet Union. Spain travelled to Moscow with high hopes for the decisive game in the group but were totally outplayed – the 2-1 defeat flattered the Spanish. The Russians confirmed their qualification with a professional if dull goalless draw in the return leg.

Belgium, a founder member of FIFA, had previously made little impression on the world stage, but as players moved from semi-professional to professional status the standard at both club and national level improved greatly. This tournament represented for them the start of an impressive series of qualifications for the final stages of major competitions. They began with three emphatic home wins against group rivals Denmark, Scotland and Portugal, and then strengthened their position with a hard-fought away victory over the Danes. Scotland won all their home legs but lost the corresponding away games, which left Portugal as the sole challenger to Belgium. Requiring a three-goal victory, Portugal threw everything, including a half-fit Eusebio, into attack against Belgium in Lisbon, but Lambert put the visitors ahead and Peres' reply from the penalty spot was of only academic interest.

World Cup runners-up and European champions Italy went through from Group Six at the expense of Austria, Sweden and the Republic of Ireland, who drew their opening game against Sweden but lost all their remaining fixtures.

In Group Seven, Yugoslavia opened their campaign with a 1-1 draw away to Holland and a 2-0 home win in the return leg. Two away victories, over East Germany and Luxembourg, put them at the top of the table. East Germany were just a point behind in second place, but defeat to the Cruyff-inspired Dutch effectively handed qualification to Yugoslavia, who needed just two points from two games, one of which was against Luxembourg. However, after having done all the hard work, the Yugoslavs nearly managed to throw it all away with 0-0 draws in both home games, against East Germany and Luxembourg respectively.

The quarter-final draw brought together Belgium and Italy, the Soviet Union and Yugoslavia, and Hungary and Romania, but the most eagerly awaited tie was between England and West Germany. In the first leg at Wembley, the Germans did not so much beat England as overwhelm them. Even though match-fixing and bribery allegations in the German Bundesliga deprived West Germany's manager, Helmut Schoen, of a number of players, any thoughts that England might gain revenge for their defeat in the 1970 World Cup quarter-final were soon dismissed. The creative alliance of Hoeness, Wimmer and Netzer in midfield created sweeping, attacking opportunites at will, and Netzer, in particular, glided around his opponents and launched out of his strolling gait into penetrative runs. One such run took him fully 50 yards before he slid the ball for Müller to attempt to squeeze in a shot which Banks did well to push wide.

Hoeness opened the scoring in the twenty-seventh minute with a 20-yard drive, and despite efforts by Lee and Peters, the Germans were soon flooding back towards Banks's goal as the first half came to an end. England started more forcefully in the second half and equalized in the seventy-sixth minute. Ball appeared to foul Wimmer, but play was waved on, and after exchanging passes with Peters, Ball struck a fierce shot which Maier could only parry to a delighted Lee, who ran it and himself into the net.

England's relief was short-lived – in fact, it lasted just seven minutes. Caught on the counter-attack, Moore's stretching attempt to tackle Held brought the German down in the penalty area. Banks got a hand to Netzer's spot-kick to push the ball on to the post but it spun behind his shoulder into the goal. Two minutes from the end Held dispossessed Hughes and passed to Hoeness, who in turn found Müller. In a fluent movement, the German striker spun and swept the ball low into the corner of the net.

The return leg lacked the inventiveness of the first as Beckenbauer marshalled his defence to achieve a rather dour 0-0 draw.

Still relatively inexperienced in major competitions, Belgium

From underdogs to champions, Laudrup celebrates Denmark's extraordinary 2-0 victory over Germany in the 1992 final in which Vilfort's goal *(below)* was also enthusiastically received by his team-mates

Before beating the Soviet Union in the 1988 final, Holland had the small matter of overcoming old adversary Germany, and here Gullit's midfield mastery and Van Basten's last-minute winner brought sweet revenge

Platini embellished the 1984 tournament with his individual skill, goals and inspirational captaincy of a great French team

Although West Germany left it late to beat the surprise package of Belgium in the 1980 final, they were certainly the best team in the tournament and deserved their second European success

Shearer's natural ability to score goals with well-timed runs into the box or thundering 30-yard drives make him one of the most dangerous and versatile strikers in the championship

Scotland will benefit from passionate support and a solid defence but will be counting on McAllister's experience, driving forward runs and blistering strikes

Del Piero, the new star of Italian football, was instrumental in Juventus' championship-winning side and has a knack of scoring spectacular goals from the left flank

Spain are a rapidly improving side and dominated their qualifying group. Athletico Madrid's Caminero provides vision, creativity and goals from midfield

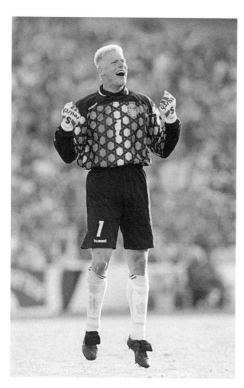

Left: Schmeichel was one of Denmark's many heroes in the 1992 championships and is a commanding influence for club and country

Below: Temperamental, unpredictable, but on his day one of the world's most gifted players, Stoichkov could still inspire Bulgaria to the heroics of USA '94

Clockwise from top left: Suker, top scorer in the qualifiers for Croatia; Hagi, massive influence in midfield for Romania; Figo, key member of a strong Portugese midfield trio; Bergkamp forms a deadly Dutch duo with Kluivert

Above: A proven goalscorer in the toughest leagues in Europe, Klinsmann was Germany's top scorer in the qualifiers and his firepower will be a key element to Germany's success

Right: Karembeu is one of the most dynamic midfielders in Europe and was outstanding in France's crucial tie against Romania capping his performance with a goal

continued to surprise. They resolutely held Italy for a well-deserved goalless draw in the away leg, and then at home, in front of a capacity crowd, Van Moer put Belgium ahead in the twenty-third minute. He suffered a broken leg following Bertini's challenge shortly before half-time. The Belgians hung on tenaciously and increased their lead in the seventy-first minute courtesy of Van Himst, and although Riva scored for Italy with a late penalty it was not enough. Belgian hobbled off worthy winners.

The Soviet Union held Yugoslavia to a goalless draw before comfortably winning their home tie 3-0. It took a third game to finally separate Hungary and Romania after two drawn games. In a close decider game Hungary joined the other semi-finalists with a goal only minutes from the end.

Belgium was chosen to host the finals and drawn to meet West Germany, Hungary playing the Soviet Union in the other semi-final.

Although they had home advantage, the Belgians were without Van Moer and were hardly a match for the Germans, whose 2-1 win did not reflect their overall superiority. Thousands of German fans travelled the short distance to Antwerp to see Müller poach two more goals, one an incredible header, before Polleunis replied for Belgium in the eighty-third minute. So West Germany were through to their first final, but Belgium had aquitted themselves very well in defeat.

By contrast, the game between Hungary and the Soviet Union was attended by only a few thousand spectators, and even they must have questioned their decision to go as the goalless first half dragged on with neither team showing much inspiration. Konkov's rising shot through a crowded goalmouth, which put the Russians on the scoresheet, was about the only attack they mustered in the second half. Thereafter they beat a retreat to defend their lead. Hungary had their chances, including a penalty which Rudakov saved from Zambo, but the cutting edge was missing and the Russians advanced to their third final in four championships.

In the third-place play-off, Hungary did manage to score from a penalty, but goals from Lambert and Van Himst gave Belgium victory.

West Germany were clear favourites to beat the Soviet Union in the final but the tournament demanded a victory with some style. The Germans did not let anyone down. From the outset, Netzer and Beckenbauer carved open the Russian defence and time and ag Rudakov was called upon to make excellent saves. At one stage

Russian goal appeared to have a charmed existence as Hoeness and Netzer saw their shots rebound off post and bar before Müller finally managed to put the Germans ahead just before half-time. In the second half, Wimmer accepted a return past from Heynckes for the second, and it was Heynckes again who inspired Müller's second and West Germany's third to round off a great performance.

The West Germans were, without doubt, the best team in Europe. Two years later they were to prove they were the best in the world.

QUALIFYING TOURNAMENT

GROUP ONE	P	W	D	L	F	A	Pts
Romania	6	4	1	1	11	2	9
Czechoslovakia	6	4	1	1	11	4	9
Wales	6	2	1	3	5	6	5
Finland	6	0	1	5	1	16	1

Czechoslovakia 1 Finland 1; Romania 3 Finland 0; Wales 0 Romania 0; Wales 1 Czechoslovakia 3; Czechoslovakia 1 Romania 0; Finland 0 Wales 1; Finland 0 Czechoslovakia 4; Finland 0 Romania 4; Wales 3 Finland 0; Czechoslovakia 1 Wales 0; Romania 2 Czechoslovakia 1; Romania 2 Wales 0

GROUP TWO	P	W	D	L	F	A	Pts
Hungary	6	4	1	1	12	5	9
Bulgaria	6	3	1	2	11	7	7
France	6	3	1	2	10	8	7
Norway	6	0	1	5	5	18	1

Norway 1 Hungary 3; France 3 Norway 1; Bulgaria 1 Norway 1; Hungary 1 France 1; Bulgaria 3 Hungary 0; Norway 1 Bulgaria 4; Norway 1 France 3; Hungary 2 Bulgaria 0; France 0 Hungary 2; ⌐gary 4 Norway 0; France 2 Bulgaria 1; Bulgaria 2 France 1

GROUP THREE	P	W	D	L	F	A	Pts
England	6	5	1	0	15	3	11
Switzerland	6	4	1	1	12	5	9
Greece	6	1	1	4	3	8	3
Malta	6	0	1	5	2	16	1

Malta 1 Greece 1; Greece 0 Switzeland 1; Malta 1 Switzerland 2;
Malta 0 England 1; England 3 Greece 0; Switzerland 5 Malta 0;
England 5 Malta 0; Switzerland 1 Greece 0; Greece 2 Malta 0;
Switzeland 2 England 3; England 1 Switzerland 1; Greece 0 England 2

GROUP FOUR	P	W	D	L	F	A	Pts
Soviet Union	6	4	2	0	13	4	10
Spain	6	3	2	1	14	3	8
Northern Ireland	6	2	2	2	10	6	6
Cyprus	6	0	0	6	2	26	0

Spain 3 Northern Ireland 0; Cyprus 0 Northern Ireland 3;
Northern Ireland 5 Cyprus 0; Cyprus 0 Spain 2; Soviet Union 2
Spain 1; Soviet Union 6 Cyprus 1; Soviet Union 1 Northern Ireland 0;
Northern Irelan 1 Soviet Union 1; Spain 0 Soviet Union 0; Cyprus 1
Soviet Union 3; Spain 7 Cyprus 0; Northern Ireland 1 Spain 1

GROUP FIVE	P	W	D	L	F	A	Pts
Belgium	6	4	1	1	11	3	9
Portugal	6	3	1	2	10	6	7
Scotland	6	3	0	3	4	7	6
Denmark	6	1	0	5	2	11	2

Denmark 0 Portugal 1; Scotland 1 Denmark 0; Belgium 2 Denmark 0;
Belgium 3 Scotland 0; Belgium 3 Portugal 0; Portugal 2 Scotland 0;
Portugal 5 Denmark 0; Denmark 1 Belgium 2; Denmark 1 Scotland 0;
Scotland 2 Portugal 1; Scotland 1 Belgium 0; Portugal 1 Belgium 1

GROUP SIX	P	W	D	L	F	A	Pts
Italy	6	4	2	0	12	4	10
Austria	6	3	1	2	14	6	7
Sweden	6	2	2	2	3	5	6
Republic of Ireland	6	0	1	5	3	17	1

Republic of Ireland 1 Sweden 1; Sweden 1 Republic of Ireland 0;
Austria 1 Italy 2; Italy 3 Republic of Ireland 0; Republic of Ireland 1
Italy 2; Sweden 1 Austria 0; Republic of Ireland 1 Austria 4; Sweden 0
Italy 0; Austria 1 Sweden 0; Italy 3 Sweden 0; Austria 6
Republic of Ireland 0; Italy 2 Austria 2

GROUP SEVEN	P	W	D	L	F	A	Pts
Yugoslavia	6	3	3	0	7	2	9
Holland	6	3	1	2	18	6	7
East Germany	6	3	1	2	11	6	7
Luxembourg	6	0	1	5	1	23	1

Holland 1 Yugoslavia 1; East Germany 1 Holland 0; Luxembourg 0
East Germany 5; Holland 6 Luxembourg 0; Yugoslavia 2 Holland 0;
East Germany 2 Luxembourg 1; East Germany 1 Yugoslavia 2;
Luxembourg 0 Yugoslavia 2; Holland 3 East Germany 2; Yugoslavia 0
East Germany 0; Yugoslavia 0 Luxembourg 0; Luxembourg 0 Holland 8

GROUP EIGHT	P	W	D	L	F	A	Pts
West Germany	6	4	2	0	10	2	10
Poland	6	2	2	2	10	6	6
Turkey	6	2	1	3	5	13	5
Albania	6	1	1	4	5	9	3

Poland 3 Albania 0; West Germany 1 Turkey 1; Turkey 2 Albania 1;
Albania 0 West Germany 1; Turkey 0 West Germany 3; Albania 1
Poland 1; West Germany 2 Albania 0; Poland 5 Turkey 1; Poland 1
West Germany 3; Albania 3 Turkey 0; West Germany 0 Poland 0;
Turkey 1 Poland 0

QUARTER-FINALS

England	1	–	3	West Germany
West Germany	0	–	0	England
Italy	0	–	0	Belgium
Belgium	2	–	0	Italy
Hungary	1	–	1	Romania
Romania	2	–	2	Hungary
Hungary	2	–	1	Romania (Belgrade)
Yugoslavia	0	–	0	Soviet Union
Soviet Union	3	–	0	Yugoslavia

SEMI-FINALS

West Germany	2	–	1	Belgium
Soviet Union	1	–	0	Hungary

THIRD-PLACE PLAY-OFF

Belgium	2	–	1	Hungary

FINAL Heysel Stadium, Brussels att: 65,000 18 June 1972

West Germany	3	–	0	Soviet Union

1976 European football had been given an enormous boost by West Germany's 1974 World Cup victory over Holland, with Poland clinching third place for good measure. And after an unpromising start, the 1976 European Championship produced standards of attacking football which have seldom been equalled in any major international tournament. To cap it all, for the fifth European Championship, a fifth different winner was crowned.

England had failed to qualify for the 1974 World Cup finals under Sir Alf Ramsey and, following Joe Mercer's short stint as caretaker manager, Ramsey had been succeeded by Don Revie. England made a promising enough start in their qualifying group with a win over Czechoslovakia at Wembley, but Revie could not steer them through to the latter stages of the tournament. They were unable to break down a tough Portuguese side at Wembley, lost away to Czechoslovakia, and in the crucial away leg in Portugal they struggled to a 1-1 draw in a game they desperately needed to win. Two victories over lightweight Cyprus, memorable only for Macdonald scoring all five goals in the Wembley match, were not enough to prevent Czechoslovakia from winning the group by a point – they had beaten the Portuguese 5-0 at home themselves.

In Group Two, Wales, drawn with Austria, Luxembourg and Hungary, got off to a losing start in Vienna against Austria, whose two second-half strikes cancelled out Griffiths' early lead. However, four wins from their next four games, against Hungary and Luxembourg, put Wales at the top of the table with Austria posing the most serious threat to their qualification. Defeat at the hands of Hungary meant that Austria needed to beat Wales in Wrexham in the group's last fixture. The Welsh required only a draw, but went one better when local favourite Griffiths scored the only goal of the game to send them through to the quarter-finals.

Wales were to be the sole British representatives in the quarter-finals. In a very competitive Group Three, Northern Ireland finished a credible second to Yugoslavia, having even topped the table for a time following an excellent 1-0 home win over the eventual group winners. This defeat aside, Yugoslavia looked ominously impressive. Scotland too faced tough opposition in Spain, Romania and Denmark. Favourites Spain began well with two away victories over

Denmark and Scotland which set them on course. The Scots regained some degree of pride with a sterling performance in the return leg, which they should have won easily. Instead they allowed the Spanish to snatch a late equalizer. Spain remained in control of the group, requiring a draw from their final game, against Romania, which they achieved, though they permitted Romania to erode a two-goal lead in the process.

Potentially the toughest group of all brought together Holland, Poland, Italy and, to make up the numbers, Finland. The Finns featured in the first three games of Group Five, losing first to Poland, then to Holland, then again to Poland. In the first decisive game of the group, Italy travelled to Holland and were holding the Dutch at 1-1 when Cruyff scored from what the Italians claimed to be an offside position. The Italians protested fervently but the goal stood and Cruyff added further salt to the Italians' wound with his second and Holland's third.

Poland could manage only a goalless draw away to Italy but then in September 1975, they produced one of the performances of the qualifying round when, in an end-to-end game, they beat a great Dutch side 4-1.

A 1-0 win away to Finland and a lacklustre goalless draw at home in the return leg had ended Italy's chances of qualification but the tussle between Poland and Holland looked set to go the distance. Following their 4-1 defeat, the Dutch had to produce something special for the return leg and they rose to the occasion. Cruyff, in particular, was inspired, and goals by Neeskens, Geels and Thijssen gave Holland a worthy victory.

Although Italy couldn't qualify themselves, they were to have a say in who did. In their last game Poland threw everything at the massed Italian defence but, as many teams have discovered at both national and club level, Italy have elevated defending into something of an art form. As a result, Holland had such a superior goal difference that they would have had to have lost by four clear goals to Italy for Poland to have pipped them to the final stages. Italy did win, but only by 1-0. Holland were through.

In the opening game of Group Six the Republic of Ireland met the mighty Soviet Union. Inspired by Giles and a hat-trick from Givens, they inflicted a stunning defeat on the group favourites. Givens was again on target to level the score against Turkey. The Republic of Ireland beat Switzerland in their next game and were leading the group when they travelled to the Soviet Union for the return leg. After their disappointing start the Russians had put together a team composed entirely of Dynamo Kiev players to beat Turkey and repeated the ploy to defeat the Irish 2-1. Three days later, the Irish were unlucky to lose to Switzerland, and although they beat Turkey 4-0, hot-shot Givens scoring all four goals, the Soviet Union needed only one point from two games to clinch the qualifying spot, which they duly did with a 4-1 win over Switzerland.

In Group Seven, the most open of the championship, Belgium, France, East Germany and Iceland slugged it out for a place in the quarter-finals. Iceland proved to be a most persistent thorn in the side of their more fancied opponents. They severely dented the prospects of both East Germany, whom they beat 2-1 at home and matched 1-1 away, and France, whom they held to a deserved draw at home. Even eventual group winners Belgium were fortunate to win both their games against Iceland.

Reigning European and world champions West Germany were drawn in Group Eight with Bulgaria, Malta and Greece. In Athens against Greece, the Germans twice went behind before scrambling a 2-2 draw. Then came a narrow 1-0 win over Malta and a 1-1 draw at home to Bulgaria. Things were not going well for the champions; Greece, despite a shock 2-0 defeat by Malta, were still in contention and in the return leg in Dusseldorf against West Germany they were unlucky not to be leading by half-time. Heynckes put the Germans ahead but Delikaris equalized and the game ended 1-1. Despite under-performing, West Germany rode their luck. A shaky 1-0 win away to Bulgaria and a comfortable 8-0 thrashing of Malta saw them through.

In the quarter-finals, Wales's brave challenge ended ingloriously against Yugoslavia in Cardiff. Having already lost 2-0 in Zagreb the previous month, on home territory they could do no more than draw 1-1. It was a match best forgotten, not so much because the Welsh were out of the competition, but because it degenerated into a bad-tempered and sometimes malicious affair compounded by inconsistent decisions from the East German referee, Rudi Gloeckner. Midway through the second half, with the score at 1-1, he disallowed Toshack's scoring shot because of dangerous play by Mahoney as he attempted a high scissors-kick. Had the goal stood, Wales would have led 2-1. At this point some Welsh supporters invaded the pitch while others threw beer bottles, cans and stones. When play resumed,

Toshack had another goal disallowed, this time for offside, but the unkindest cut of all came five minutes from the end, when Maric saved Yorath's anxious penalty kick. The referee was given a police escort as he left the field.

West Germany drew 1-1 with Spain in Madrid and went through to meet Yugoslavia in the semi-finals following a 2-0 win in Munich. Sound in defence and inventive in attack, the Germans were finding their form at the right time.

Neither did the Dutch have too much difficulty reaching the semi-finals. Their 2-1 win over Belgium gave them an overwhelming 7-1 aggregate, Holland having won the opening leg 5-0 in Rotterdam.

Czechoslovakia claimed the fourth semi-final place thanks to an impressive 2-0 victory over the Soviet Union in the home leg and a battling 2-2 draw in the return game, in which Moder scored both Czech goals.

Yugoslavia was selected to host the final stages and were drawn to play West Germany in Belgrade. With Czechoslovakia meeting Holland in the other semi, the stage looked set for a repeat of the memorable 1974 World Cup final, in which West Germany had beaten Holland 2-1.

Played in driving rain, the game between Czechoslovakia and Holland was nevertheless a match of high quality. Ondrus opened the scoring in the twentieth minute when he headed in Panenka's cross to put the Czechs ahead. It was a lead they held until fifteen minutes from the end of normal time when, ironically, Ondrus deflected a fast centre from Geels into his own net. Although the game was far from unpleasant or cynical, the Czech midfielder, Pollak, had earlier been sent off by referee Clive Thomas for a foul on Neeskens and twelve minutes from time Neeskens himself was sent off for a nasty tackle on Nehoda.

Rensenbrink went close for Holland, drawing fine saves from Viktor, but the game was forced into extra time. With just seven minutes remaining and a penalty shoot-out looming Dutch superstar Cruyff appeared to be fouled by Panenka. However, Thomas waved play on and the Czechs mounted a counter-attack from which Nehoda scored. The Dutch were livid and Van Hanegem became the third player to get an early bath, in his case for dissent. Vesely scored a third Czech goal two minutes from time. In spite of the dreadful playing conditions, both teams had displayed a level of technique and skill admired by all who sat absorbed by the match for two hours. But in the end it was greater unity and spirit that saw Czechoslovakia home against a talented Dutch side whose ranks were broken by dissension.

The next day the holders, West Germany, took on hosts Yugoslavia. Urged on by the partisan crowd, Yugoslavia simply tore into the German defence, overwhelming them with the sheer invention of their approach play, particularly down each flank. On the left, Dzajic produced a series of crosses which any number of his colleagues were ready to collect. Maier made a succession of fine saves in the German goal, but he was beaten when Popivoda swept in a superb pass from Oblak. Yugoslavia continued to torment the Germans and Dzajic drove home their second in the thirty-second minute as time and again the home side ripped through the German defence.

The game could have been all over by the start of the second half had Yugoslavia not given their opponents the time to regroup. In the sixty-fourth minute German substitute Flohe drove home Hoeness's pass. West Germany's traditional resilience had once again been a major factor and a second inspired substitution by manager Helmut Schoen proved decisive. With ten minutes to go he sent on Dieter Müller for his international debut, and with his first touch the newcomer headed in the equalizer from Bonhof's corner kick to take the game into extra time. Popivoda forced a remarkable save from Maier, but with six minutes remaining, Müller fired in his second. Two minutes from time he completed an amazing hat-trick to complete an astonishing about-turn.

The hosts now faced Holland, who were without the suspended Cruyff and Neeskens, to play off for third place in a match which was another fine display of attacking football. Geels and Willy van der Kerkhoff put the Dutch ahead, Katalinski pulling one back for Yugoslavia just before half-time. With a minute of normal time remaining, Dzajic levelled the score from a free kick to send the game into extra time. Yugoslavia had their chances, but it was Holland who claimed third place with a second goal for Geels.

After three such high-quality and dramatic games, one wondered if the bubble might just burst before the final itself. There was no need to worry: the final turned out to be the best game of them all.

Czechoslovakia took the lead after just eight minutes after one of their bewildering cross-field moves. Maier parried a shot by Gogh,

Nehoda centred and Svehlick drove into an empty net. After 25 minutes, the Czechs were two up. The inspirational Masny took a free kick which was cleared by Beckenbauer, only for Dobias to shoot home from 20 yards. But the Germans were nothing if not resilient and within three minutes semi-final hat-trick hero Müller had volleyed them back into the match. The score remained at 2-1 until the very last touch of normal time, when, as the Germans attacked desperately and had, it seemed, been denied by Viktor, up popped Holzenbein to head in Bonhof's corner. The great survivors had done it again, forcing the fourth game of the week into extra time.

Now it was West Germany who looked most likely to win, but Viktor pulled out at least six world-class saves and the Czechs always remained dangerous on the counter-attack. After a week of fascinating football the champions had finally to be decided by penalty kicks. The suspense was unbearable as Masny, Nehoda, Ondrus and Jurkemik converted their spot-kicks for Czechoslovakia while Bonhof, Flohe and Bongartz replied for West Germany. Hoeness stepped up for the eighth kick and put his shot over the bar. Panenka chipped his coolly over Maier and Czechoslovakia were the new European champions.

QUALIFYING TOURNAMENT

GROUP ONE	P	W	D	L	F	A	Pts
Czechoslovakia	6	4	1	1	15	5	9
England	6	3	2	1	11	3	8
Portugal	6	2	3	1	5	7	7
Cyprus	6	0	0	6	0	16	0

England 3 Czechoslovakia 0; England 0 Portugal 0; England 5
Cyprus 0; Czechoslovakia 4 Cyprus 0; Czechoslovakia 5 Portugal 0;
Cyprus 0 England 1; Cyprus 0 Portugal 2; Czechoslovakia 2 England 1;
Portugal 1 Czechoslovakia 1; Portugal 1 England 1; Cyprus 0
Czechoslovakia 3; Portugal 1 Cyprus 0

GROUP TWO	P	W	D	L	F	A	Pts
Wales	6	5	0	1	14	4	10
Hungary	6	3	1	2	15	8	7
Austria	6	3	1	2	11	7	7
Luxembourg	6	0	0	6	7	28	0

Austria 2 Wales 1; Luxembourg 2 Hungary 4; Wales 2 Hungary 0;
Wales 5 Luxembourg 0; Luxembourg 1 Austria 2; Austria 0 Hungary 0;
Hungary 1 Wales 2; Luxembourg 1 Wales 3; Hungary 2 Austria 1;
Austria 6 Luxembourg 2; Hungary 8 Luxembourg 1; Wales 1 Austria 0

GROUP THREE	P	W	D	L	F	A	Pts
Yugoslavia	6	5	0	1	12	4	10
Northern Ireland	6	3	0	3	8	5	6
Sweden	6	3	0	3	8	9	6
Norway	6	1	0	5	5	15	2

Norway 2 Northern Ireland 1; Yugoslavia 3 Norway 1; Sweden 0
Northern Ireland 2; Northern Ireland 1 Yugoslavia 0; Sweden 1
Yugoslavia 2; Norway 1 Yugoslavia 3; Sweden 3 Norway 1; Norway 0
Sweden 2; Northern Ireland 1 Sweden 2; Yugoslavia 3 Sweden 0;
Northern Ireland 3 Norway 0; Yugoslavia 1 Northern Ireland 0

GROUP FOUR	P	W	D	L	F	A	Pts
Spain	6	3	3	0	10	6	9
Romania	6	1	5	0	11	6	7
Scotland	6	2	3	1	8	6	7
Denmark	6	0	1	5	3	14	1

Denmark 1 Spain 2; Denmark 0 Romania 0; Scotland 1 Spain 2;
Spain 1 Scotland 1; Spain 1 Romania 1; Romania 6 Denmark 1;
Romania 1 Scotland 1; Denmark 0 Scotland 1; Spain 2 Denmark 0;
Scotland 3 Denmark 1; Romania 2 Spain 2; Scotland 1 Romania 1

GROUP FIVE	P	W	D	L	F	A	Pts
Holland	6	4	0	2	14	8	8
Poland	6	3	2	1	9	5	8
Italy	6	2	3	1	3	3	7
Finland	6	0	1	5	3	13	1

Finland 1 Poland 2; Finland 1 Holland 2; Poland 3 Finland 0; Holland 3
Italy 1; Italy 0 Poland 0; Finland 0 Italy 1; Holland 4 Finland 1;
Poland 4 Holland 1; Italy 0 Finland 0; Holland 3 Poland 0; Poland 0
Italy 0; Italy 1 Holland 0

GROUP SIX	P	W	D	L	F	A	Pts
Soviet Union	6	4	0	2	10	6	8
Republic of Ireland	6	3	1	2	11	5	7
Turkey	6	2	2	2	5	10	6
Switzerland	6	1	1	4	5	10	3

Republic of Ireland 3 Soviet Union 0; Turkey 1 Republic of Ireland 1;
Turkey 2 Switzerland 1; Soviet Union 3 Turkey 0; Switzerland 1
Turkey 1; Republic of Ireland 2 Switzerland 1; Soviet Union 2
Republic of Ireland 1; Switzerland 1 Republic of Ireland 0; Switzerland 0
Soviet Union 1; Republic of Ireland 4 Turkey 0; Soviet Union 4
Switzerland 1; Turkey 1 Soviet Union 0

GROUP SEVEN	P	W	D	L	F	A	Pts
Belgium	6	3	2	1	6	3	8
East Germany	6	2	3	1	8	7	7
France	6	1	3	2	7	6	5
Iceland	6	1	2	3	3	8	4

Iceland 0 Belgium 2; East Germany 1 Iceland 1; Belgium 2 France 1;
France 2 East Germany 2; East Germany 0 Belgium 0; Iceland 0 France 0;
Iceland 2 East Germany 1; France 3 Iceland 0; Belgium 1 Iceland 0;
Belgium 1 East Germany 2; East Germany 2 France 1; France 0 Belgium 0

GROUP EIGHT	P	W	D	L	F	A	Pts
West Germany	6	3	3	0	14	4	9
Greece	6	2	3	1	12	9	7
Bulgaria	6	2	2	2	12	7	6
Malta	6	1	0	5	2	20	2

Bulgaria 3 Greece 3; Greece 2 West Germany 2; Greece 2 Bulgaria 1;
Malta 0 West Germany 1; Malta 2 Greece 0; Bulgaria 1
West Germany 1; Greece 4 Malta 0; Bulgaria 5 Malta 0;
West Germany 1 Greece 1; West Germany 1 Bulgaria 0; Malta 0
Bulgaria 2; West Germany 8 Malta 0

QUARTER-FINALS

Czechoslovakia	2 – 0	Soviet Union
Soviet Union	2 – 2	Czechoslovakia
Holland	5 – 0	Belgium
Belgium	1 – 2	Holland
Yugoslavia	2 – 0	Wales
Wales	1 – 1	Yugoslavia
Spain	1 – 1	West Germany
West Germany	2 – 0	Spain

SEMI-FINALS

Czechoslovakia	3 – 1	Holland (aet)
West Germany	4 – 2	Yugoslavia (aet)

THIRD-PLACE PLAY-OFF

Holland	3 – 2	Yugoslavia (aet)

FINAL Zvezda, Belgrade att: 45,000 20 June 1976

Czechoslovakia 2 – 2 West Germany
(Czechoslovakia won 5 – 3 on penalties)

1980   On its return to Italy, a new format was adopted for the championship. The formula which had produced such outstanding matches four years earlier was cast aside and for many observers this contributed to some negative, cautious games. In fairness, however, it would have been difficult for any tournament to match the four memorable games from the 1976 championship involving Czechoslovakia, West Germany, Holland and Yugoslavia for excitement and drama.

For this championship the quarter-finals were scrapped in favour of a system whereby the seven group winners from the qualifying rounds proceeded to a final tournament which consisted of two four-team groups, the winners of each contesting the final. The hosts, Italy, were chosen from the outset rather than after the quarter-finals, as had been the case in previous tournaments, and were also given a bye to the final stages.

The format of the championship might have changed, but the old order was maintained as West Germany, the outstanding team in European football for a decade, reached their third consecutive European Championship final. In the qualifying round, the Germans, under new manager Jupp Derwall, initially struggled to find a goal-scoring successor to Müller, but after goalless draws with Malta and Turkey they won all their subsequent group games, ending Welsh hopes along the way with a 5-1 victory in Cologne.

A car crash had cost Derwall one of the safest pairs of hands in the game – Maier's – and the team also lost star striker Fischer with a broken leg shortly before the finals. But the Germans could count on the precocious if erratic Hansi Müller, and the Bundesliga's top marksman, Rummenigge.

The new format appeared to favour teams playing the percentage game – making sure they did not lose to their nearest group rivals and scoring as heavily as possible against the weaker opponents. If the competition was to emulate its immediate predecessor, this showcase of European football desperately needed teams to play positive, attacking football. It did not help matters that the European Championship was deprived of two other potential stars before it had even started.

England, under Ron Greenwood, were cursing the absence

through an Achilles' injury of their key striker, Francis. On the positive side, they had qualified for their first major international tournament since 1970 without being beaten and had established a consistency of performance which gave considerable cause for optimism.

The other influential player to miss the finals was Italy's brilliant striker, Rossi, who was banned following domestic bribery and match-fixing allegations which rocked Italian football. Investigators eventually dropped charges against Juventus but the whole episode undoubtedly affected the national side's morale. Still, they could still include players of great ability such as Tardelli, Scirea, Antognoni and Zoff to outweigh this setback.

The holders of the trophy, Czechoslovakia, qualified for the final stages at the expense of France and, with the notable exception of their goalkeeping saviour from the 1976 final, Viktor, many of their influential players – Ondrus and Jurkemik in defence, Panenka in midfield and Masny and Nehoda in attack – remained. They were drawn in Group One with West Germany, Holland and Greece.

After reaching a second consecutive World Cup final in 1978 the Dutch were now without Neeskens, Cruyff or Rensenbrink. But as they showed in Leipzig when they recovered from 2-0 down to defeat East Germany in the decisive qualifying game, they were not to be dismissed lightly. The Van de Kerkhof twins, Rep and Haan, and the elegant sweeper Krol, who was as instrumental in attack as in defence, formed the core of an accomplished and capable team.

The Greeks had overcome both Hungary and the Soviet Union to qualify for their first-ever finals but this was, at the time, more a reflection of the poor state of Soviet and Hungarian football than of a dramatic improvement by Greece.

In Group Two, England and Italy were joined by Belgium and Spain. Belgium were very much the dark horses of the competition. They had qualified from a formidable group which contained Portugal, Austria, Scotland and Norway with an impressive late surge. The thirty-four-year-old midfielder Van Moer returned to provide an experienced head to marshal a side which boasted excellent forwards in Van den Bergh, Ceulemans and the ubiquitous Van der Elst, who could provide the speed, accuracy and dedicated running to expose opponents.

Spain had done well to overcome Yugoslavia and Romania to win their qualifying group but manager Kubala's attempt at a youth policy hadn't worked. He reinstated veteran midfielders Asensi and Cardenosa to the squad. Arconada was considered Europe's top goal-keeper but it looked as though he would be given plenty of opportunities to prove it.

The two opening games of the finals were played on the same day and both featured the Group One teams. In a replay of the 1976 final, West Germany took on Czechoslovakia and a relatively cautious game before a pitifully small crowd only sprung into life once Rummenigge had given the Germans a fifty-fifth-minute lead. There was no further score. Holland met newcomers Greece in Naples and gratefully accepted both points when the Greek goalkeeper, Konstantinou, needlessly gave away a penalty which Kist converted.

For their crucial game against Holland, the Germans decided to use a genuine centre forward, Hrubesch, and his presence caused problems in the Dutch defence from the start. After nineteen minutes, Schuster drove a fierce shot against the post giving Allofs the easiest of goals. On the hour, Schuster, the source of numerous inventive moves, found Müller who rolled the ball into the path of Allofs to shoot low past Schrijvers. Remarkably, Allofs completed his hat-trick seven minutes later and once again it was Schuster who created the chance with a glorious run and pass.

Holland, belatedly, came to life scoring two unexpected goals. The first came after seventy-five minutes when Wijnstekers was brought down for a penalty which Rep converted. A blistering strike from Willy van der Kerkhof brought the game into Holland's reach in the eighty-sixth minute, but they had left it too late.

Czechoslovakia defeated Greece 3-1 on the same day – although the Greeks again proved they were no lightweights – and three days later they faced Holland. Both sides knew that West Germany were virtually assured of their place in the final. Withstanding early Dutch pressure, Czechoslovakia took the lead through a close-range effort from Nehoda and looked the most likely side to score again as they mounted rapier-like counter-attacks.

Holland brought on Haan, who forced Netolicka into two fine saves with thunderous drives, and Kist, who fired in the equalizer in the fifty-eighth minute. Thereafter both sides became involved in niggly fouls and the Turkish referee was kept busy right up to the final whistle.

The result confirmed West Germany's place in the final before they took the field against Greece and so they reorganized their team to rest players and to avoid the risk of more bookings and suspensions. Greece made a brave fist of it and came close on a number of occasions in a goalless draw.

Group Two started with a game between England and Belgium in Turin. The Belgians had beaten England only once in sixteen games and when Wilkins gave the favourites the lead with a superb goal English optimism seemed justified. Six minutes later, however, Ceulemans equalized, whereupon a riot broke out on the terraces between local fans and England supporters. The game was held up for five minutes while Clemence and several other players recovered from the effects of police tear gas. When play resumed the zest had deserted England, and neither side added to the score.

Italy opened their campaign in Milan with their own fans chanting abuse at the team and manager, Enzo Bearzot. They struggled to hold unfancied Spain and the game ended goalless. Three days later in Turin, Tardelli's goal for Italy eleven minutes from time put paid to English hopes of reaching the final. It turned out to be the only goal the Italians were to score in the group matches but the fact remained that, apart from Kennedy's shot which hit the angle of bar and post, England did not seriously disturb the Italian goal and had to withstand concerted pressure throughout the second half, on which Antognoni exerted a leading influence for the Italians.

Earlier the same day, Belgium had moved to the top of the group with a 2-1 win over Spain who, despite their wealth of possession, were all too often caught out by the Belgians' ability to counter-attack. Ceulemans was inspirational in this respect, his all-round strength and incisive running instigating the first goal, scored by Gerets. Although Quini equalized, it was Ceulemans' strength and tenacity which set up the pass for Cools to score the winner. Before the tournament, the Belgian coach, Guy Thys, had said: 'If we avoid defeat against England and beat Spain, anything is possible.' It was starting to look as if it was.

England salvaged some pride by beating Spain 2-1, but the deciding game was in Rome, where the Italians, who had the same goal difference as Belgium but only one goal to their credit, needed to win. In what turned out to be a somewhat ill-tempered affair, Belgium were never seriously troubled and held the increasingly desperate Italians to a goalless draw.

Belgium's unexpected appearance in the final in Rome gave it a certain curiosity value even though the Germans were expected to win comfortably. West Germany took an early lead through Hrubesch after ten minutes and proceeded to dominate the first half, Schuster once again proving an inventive and important figure. But the Belgians slowly recovered and Ceulemans in particular looked dangerous, despite a lack of support. With seventy minutes gone Stielike's challenge tripped Van der Elst in what looked to be just outside the penalty area. However, the Romanian referee pointed to the spot and Van der Eycken calmly brought the scores level with a neatly placed spot-kick.

As extra time loomed it was the young German side that looked most vulnerable, but with just three minutes remaining Hrubesch rose to meet Rummenigge's corner with a header to end the Belgian revival in what seemed to be an almost customary West German habit of leaving it to the very last moment.

After a series of largely over-cautious games, the championship was at least partly redeemed by an exciting climax and the young German side deserved their triumph.

QUALIFYING TOURNAMENT

GROUP ONE	P	W	D	L	F	A	Pts
England	8	7	1	0	22	5	15
Northern Ireland	8	4	1	3	8	14	9
Republic of Ireland	8	2	3	3	9	8	7
Bulgaria	8	2	1	5	6	14	5
Denmark	8	1	2	5	13	17	4

Denmark 3 Republic of Ireland 3; Republic of Ireland 0
Northern Ireland 0; Denmark 3 England 4; Denmark 2 Bulgaria 2;
Republic of Ireland 1 England 1; Northern Ireland 2 Denmark 1;
Bulgaria 0 Northern Ireland 2; England 4 Northern Ireland 0;
Republic of Ireland 2 Denmark 0; Northern Ireland 2 Bulgaria 0;
Bulgaria 1 Republic of Ireland 0; Bulgaria 0 England 3; Denmark 4
Northern Ireland 0; England 1 Denmark 0; Republic of Ireland 3
Bulgaria 0; Northern Ireland 1 England 5; Bulgaria 3 Denmark 0;
England 2 Bulgaria 0; Northern Ireland 1 Republic of Ireland 0;
England 2 Republic of Ireland 0

GROUP TWO	**P**	**W**	**D**	**L**	**F**	**A**	**Pts**
Belgium	8	4	4	0	12	5	12
Austria	8	4	3	1	14	7	11
Portugal	8	4	1	3	10	11	9
Scotland	8	3	1	4	15	13	7
Norway	8	0	1	7	5	20	1

Norway 0 Austria 2; Belgium 1 Norway 1; Austria 3 Scotland 2;
Portugal 1 Belgium 1; Scotland 3 Norway 2; Austria 1 Portugal 2;
Portugal 1 Scotland 0; Scotland 1 Belgium 3; Belgium 1 Austria 1;
Austria 0 Belgium 0; Norway 0 Portugal 1; Norway 0 Scotland 4;
Austria 4 Norway 0; Norway 1 Belgium 2; Belgium 2 Portugal 0;
Scotland 1 Austria 1; Portugal 3 Norway 1; Belgium 2 Scotland 0;
Portugal 0 Austria 2; Scotland 4 Portugal 1

GROUP THREE	**P**	**W**	**D**	**L**	**F**	**A**	**Pts**
Spain	6	4	1	1	13	5	9
Yugoslavia	6	4	0	2	14	6	8
Romania	6	2	2	2	9	8	6
Cyprus	6	0	1	5	2	19	1

Yugoslavia 1 Spain 2; Romania 3 Yugoslavia 2; Spain 1 Romania 0;
Spain 5 Cyprus 0; Cyprus 0 Yugoslavia 3; Romania 2 Spain 2;
Cyprus 1 Romania 1; Spain 0 Yugoslavia 1; Yugoslavia 2 Romania 1;
Yugoslavia 5 Cyprus 0; Romania 2 Cyprus 0; Cyprus 1 Spain 3

GROUP FOUR	**P**	**W**	**D**	**L**	**F**	**A**	**Pts**
Holland	8	6	1	1	20	6	13
Poland	8	5	2	1	13	4	12
East Germany	8	5	1	2	18	11	11
Switzerland	8	2	0	6	7	18	4
Iceland	8	0	0	8	2	21	0

Iceland 0 Poland 2; Holland 3 Iceland 0; East Germany 3 Iceland 1;
Switzerland 1 Holland 3; Holland 3 East Germany 0; Poland 2
Switzerland 0; Holland 3 Switzerland 0; East Germany 2 Poland 1;
Poland 2 Holland 0; Switzerland 0 East Germany 2; Switzerland 2
Iceland 0; Iceland 1 Switzerland 2; Iceland 0 Holland 4; Iceland 0
East Germany 3; Switzerland 0 Poland 2; Poland 1 EastGermany 1;
Poland 2 Iceland 0; East Germany 5 Switzerland 2; Holland 1 Poland 1;
East Germany 2 Holland 3

GROUP FIVE	P	W	D	L	F	A	Pts
Czechoslovakia	6	5	0	1	17	4	10
France	6	4	1	1	13	7	9
Sweden	6	1	2	3	9	13	4
Luxembourg	6	0	1	5	2	17	1

France 2 Sweden 2; Sweden 1 Czechoslovakia 3; Luxembourg 1
France 3; France 3 Luxembourg 0; Czechoslovakia 2 France 0;
Luxembourg 0 Czechoslovakia 3; Sweden 3 Luxembourg 0; Sweden 1
France 3; Czechoslovakia 4 Sweden 1; Luxembourg 1 Sweden 1;
France 2 Czechoslovakia 1; Czechoslovakia 4 Luxembourg 0

GROUP SIX	P	W	D	L	F	A	Pts
Greece	6	3	1	2	13	7	7
Hungary	6	2	2	2	9	9	6
Finland	6	2	2	2	10	15	6
Soviet Union	6	1	3	2	7	8	5

Finland 3 Greece 0; Finland 2 Hungary 1; Soviet Union 2 Greece 0;
Hungary 2 Soviet Union 0; Greece 8 Finland 1; Greece 4 Hungary 1;
Hungary 0 Greece 0; Soviet Union 2 Hungary 2; Finland 1 Soviet Union 1;
Greece 1 Soviet Union 0; Hungary 3 Finland 1; Soviet Union 2 Finland 2

GROUP SEVEN	P	W	D	L	F	A	Pts
West Germany	6	4	2	0	17	1	10
Turkey	6	3	1	2	5	5	7
Wales	6	3	0	3	11	8	6
Malta	6	0	1	5	2	21	1

Wales 7 Malta 0; Wales 1 Turkey 0; Malta 0 West Germany 0;
Turkey 2 Malta 1; Turkey 0 West Germany 0; Wales 0
West Germany 2; Malta 0 Wales 2; West Germany 5 Wales 1;
Malta 1 Turkey 2; Turkey 1 Wales 0; West Germany 2 Turkey 0;
West Germany 8 Malta 0

Italy qualified as hosts

FINAL TOURNAMENT. 11-22 JUNE 1980

GROUP ONE	P	W	D	L	F	A	Pts
West Germany	3	2	1	0	4	2	5
Czechoslovakia	3	1	1	1	4	3	3
Holland	3	1	1	1	4	4	3
Greece	3	0	1	2	1	4	1

West Germany 1 Czechoslvakia 0; Holland 1 Greece 0;
West Germany 3 Holland 2; Czechoslovakia 3 Greece 1;
Czechoslovakia 1 Holland 1; West Germany 0 Greece 0

GROUP TWO	P	W	D	L	F	A	Pts
Belgium	3	1	2	0	3	2	4
Italy	3	1	2	0	1	0	4
England	3	1	1	1	3	3	3
Spain	3	0	1	2	2	4	1

Belgium 1 England 1; Italy 0 Spain 0; Spain 1 Belgium 2;
Italy 1 England 0; Italy 0 Belgium 0; England 2 Spain 1

THIRD-PLACE PLAY-OFF

Czechoslovakia 1 – 1   Italy (9-8 pens)

FINAL Olympic Stadium, Rome att: 48,000 22 June 1980

West Germany   2 – 1   Belgium

1984

France, under the inspiration of Platini, restored the spirit of 1976 to the European Championship with a series of marvellous performances. Platini was undoubtedly the player of the finals, but France's triumph was as much a victory for the game as it was for the host nation. The finals were enthusiastically supported by good-natured crowds and the success of the tournament totally justified the decision to choose France as hosts. The French built new stadia and renovated older ones in preparation for the competition and football fans were treated to a well-organized and entertaining championship. The French team, in particular, were outstanding and their victory partially compensated for their unlucky and controversial defeat by West Germany in the 1982 World Cup semi-final.

Some of the key teams failing to qualify for the 1984 finals included Scotland, England, the Soviet Union, Wales, Italy and Holland. Although Scotland finished bottom of their qualifying group, England were expected to do well and started their campaign in Group Three with a draw away to Denmark and a 3-0 win over Greece. A 9-0 defeat of Luxembourg – which included a hat-trick from Luther Blissett on his first full appearance for England – provided a healthy goal tally, but a dropped point against Greece was disappointing and potentially disastrous. And so it proved. Victory over Hungary put England at the top of the table but Denmark – a strong emerging football nation with such talented players as Olsen, Laudrup, Elkjaer and Lerby – were serious challengers. The crunch game at Wembley in September 1983 saw the Danes in positive, attacking mood and when Neal handled the ball in the area Simonsen strode up to put Denmark ahead in the game and the group. Denmark's surprising defeat by Hungary gave England a glimmer of hope, but the Danes ensured qualification, by one point, by beating Greece in Athens.

In Group Four, Wales also failed to qualify for the finals by a solitary point. Having beaten Norway and Bulgaria and drawn an entertaining 4-4 goal-fest of a game against Yugoslavia, they could manage only two points from their next three matches. However, they still topped the table and nearest challengers Yugoslavia needed to win their final game against Bulgaria by two clear goals to overtake them. Welsh hopes were raised when Bulgaria opened the scoring, but Susic levelled matters and then went on to put Yugoslavia ahead.

Still they required another goal, and deep into injury time defender Radanovic rose to the challenge to head his team into the finals.

Northern Ireland were denied a place in the finals by West Germany, but again it was a close call. Having been beaten only once by a European team in the previous four years, West Germany, reigning European champions and strong favourites to retain the title, were expected to qualify from Group Six with ease. But in two extraordinary performances Northern Ireland beat them twice – 1-0 on both occasions. Had it not been for a defeat against Turkey, Northern Ireland would surely have qualified, and deservedly so. As it was, they went out on goal difference.

But the most amazing qualification for the 1984 finals, and perhaps of all finals, involved the group containing Spain and Holland. The two countries were level going into the concluding group games. Each had beaten the other at home and drawn another fixture, but Holland had such a superior goal difference that Spain would need to defeat Malta, their last opponents, by eleven clear goals to displace Holland as qualifiers. The game started badly for Spain when Señor missed an early penalty, but Santillana put them ahead after fifteen minutes, only for Malta to equalize. Two more goals for Spain before half-time did not appear to be sufficient but in an incredible second half the Maltese lost confidence and morale and conceded a glut of goals. Señor made up for his earlier miss to score Spain's twelfth and last goal to send them through to the finals.

Accompanying West Germany, Denmark, Yugoslavia and Spain to the European Championship finals were Belgium, Romania, and Portugal, who had qualified for the first time at the expense of the Soviet Union.

France qualified automatically as hosts and faced Denmark, Belgium and Yugoslavia in Group One of the finals. European champions West Germany were drawn against Spain, Romania and Portugal in Group Two.

The deciding stages got underway when the hosts met Denmark in Paris in a match which illustrated the best and worst aspects of the game. Both sides played open and attacking football, Denmark's fluent attacking style relying on just three defenders for most of the time. The match was finely balanced, but shortly before half-time a collision between Le Roux and Simonsen left the Danish former European Footballer of the Year with a badly broken leg.

The French began to take control in the second half and in the seventy-seventh minute a swift build-up involving Giresse and Tigana allowed Platini to fire the French ahead from the edge of the area. In a desperate late gamble, the Danes sent on Olsen, who was head-butted by Amoros. The French defender was sent off and later received a three-match suspension, but the French had overcome a tough hurdle.

Belgium had opened their account with a 2-0 win over Yugoslavia, masterminded by the flowering talents of the eighteen-year-old Scifo, but he was totally overshadowed in their second game as a rampant French team beat them 5-0. Platini gave France an early lead and their irresistible attacking overwhelmed Belgium. France were 3-0 up at half-time, and in the eighty-eighth minute Platini scored a fourth from the penalty spot to complete his hat-trick with France's fifth.

On the same day as Belgium were being beaten 5-0 by the hosts, Yugoslavia were suffering the same fate against Denmark in Lyons. In a thrilling game the Danes displayed their trademark pace and power to stunning effect.

As the top two clubs from each table qualified for the semi-finals, France, with two victories, were already assured of their place. Yugoslavia were also assured of their fate – elimination – and the encounter was played at a more relaxed pace. Yugoslavia took the lead through Sestic on the half-hour, but Platini, Giresse and Tigana looking unstoppable, and fifteen minutes into the second half Platini, inevitably, unleashed the first goal of a second brilliant hat-trick to take France through to the semis.

Denmark needed only to draw against Belgium in order to book the second semi-final spot, but true to style they refused to play defensively and attacked from the start. This tactic began to look somewhat naive when Belgium took the lead through Ceulemans and extended it in the thirty-eighth minute through Vercauteren. Two minutes later Arnesen cut the deficit from the penalty spot and fifteen minutes into the second half Brylle restored parity. Although Belgium had their chances, it was left to Elkjaer to seal a 3-2 win for Denmark seven minutes from time.

If Group One had witnessed a plethora of excitement and goals, Group Two was a totally different game of soldiers. In total, Group One yielded twenty-three goals from six matches; Group Two managed a paltry nine.

West Germany faced Portugal in their opening group game and a dour, defensive contest ensued, with the Portuguese playing defensively. In the first half, West Germany pulled Rummenigge back into midfield, which severely reduced their attacking options. Not until he moved back into attack in the second did West Germany threaten the Portuguese goal, but the match remained goalless. Later that day, Spain drew 1-1 with Romania in an equally uninspiring game.

In their next encounter, against Romania, the West Germans appeared to be back on their normal successful course and recorded a 2-1 victory. While they looked every inch the winners at half-time, they did concede an equalizer, but Voller restored their advantage with his and West Germany's second goal. Spain and Portugal drew 1-1 in Marseilles. Going into the finals matches, all four countries were in contention for a place in the semi-finals.

Despite losing their key player, Chalana, early on, Portugal took the game to Romania and veteran Benfica striker Nene scored an excellent winner. Over in Paris, West Germany appeared to be cruising but although they had the edge over Spain the match remained goalless until the final minute, when in a desperate last attack Maceda headed home to take Spain into the semis to meet Denmark.

In the semi-finals, France met Portugal in Marseilles and Spain played Denmark in Lyons. In the early part of their game the French were matched stride for stride by the Portuguese, with Chalana, in particular, a constant threat. After twenty-four minutes the hosts took the lead when Domergue lashed in a free kick, but it wasn't until the second half that they started to improve and create chances. With fifteen minutes to go, Jordao headed in the equalizer from the influential Chalana's cross. After the French hit the bar, extra time beckoned.

In extra time Chalana was just as menacing. Jordao mis-hit Chalana's cross, but then watched as it bounced over Bats' head into the French goal. For many other teams this would have been the killer blow, and some French heads did drop, but their attacking spirit was irrepressible. Fernandez, Bossis and Tigana swept forward, and with just six minutes remaining, Domergue scored his second. Refusing to sit back and defend, the French pushed on and in the final minute they were rewarded when Tigana put Platini through to score the winner which set car horns blaring all night.

In the other semi-final, which took place the following day, the previously maligned Spanish side deservedly secured their berth in the final – even if they did so by the unsatisfactory adjudication of a penalty shoot-out. Denmark had started brightly, Lerby scoring after just six minutes, but as the match progressed the Spanish steadily improved until Maceda drilled home the equalizer after sixty-seven minutes. Elkjaer, one of the outstanding players of the tournament, made the crucial miss at 4-4 and Spain progressed to their second championship final. But it was at considerable cost: they would be without Gordillo and Maceda, both of whom were booked by the English referee, George Courtney.

The Danes had won many admirers for their entertaining style of football and were to continue their progress with qualification for the 1986 World Cup and a memorable 6-1 victory over Uruguay.

After their imperious progress to the final, it was perhaps asking too much of manager Hidalgo's team of French artisans to play with the same elan that had characterized their performances in the early rounds. As it was, Spain demonstrated that they too could play intelligent, accurate football coupled with what might euphemistically be termed over-zealous tackling. For much of the final's opening half, France struggled to compete tactically and physically, and it was Spain, tight in defence and penetrating on the counter-attack, who looked more dangerous.

Czech referee Christov booked Gallego and Garrasco of Spain in the first half-hour, but ironically, when France's opening came in the fifty-seventh minute, it was from a questionable free kick. It helped to give Platini his ninth and most critical goal of the tournament. He bent the kick around the Spanish wall, and as goalkeeper Arconada dived to collect the ball he allowed it to sneak under him and over the line.

Spain continued to search for the goal which might send the game into extra time and with four minutes to go French nerves were set jangling when Le Roux was sent off for a second bookable offence. But as Spain pressed forward Tigana released Bellone to score France's second and crown their hour of glory in the last minute.

QUALIFYING TOURNAMENT

GROUP ONE	P	W	D	L	F	A	Pts
Belgium	6	4	1	1	12	8	9
Switzerland	6	2	2	2	7	9	6
East Germany	6	2	1	3	7	7	5
Scotland	6	1	2	3	8	10	4

Belgium 3 Switzerland 0; Scotland 2 East Germany 0; Switzerland 2
Scotland 0; Belgium 3 Scotland 2; Scotland 2 Switzerland 2;
East Germany 1 Belgium 2; Belgium 2 East Germany 1; Switzerland 0
East Germany 0; Scotland 1 Belgium 1; Wast Germany 3 Switzerland 0;
Switzerland 3 Belgium 1; East Germany 2 Scotland 1

GROUP TWO	P	W	D	L	F	A	Pts
Portugal	6	5	0	1	11	6	10
Soviet Union	6	4	1	1	11	2	9
Poland	6	1	2	3	6	9	4
Finland	6	0	1	5	3	14	1

Finland 2 Poland 3; Finland 0 Portugal 2; Portugal 2 Poland 1;
Soviet Umnion 2 Finland 0; Poland 1 Finland 1; Soviet Union 5
Portugal 0; Poland 1 Soviet Union 1; Finland 0 Soviet Union 1;
Portugal 5 Finland 0; Soviet Union 2 Poland 0; Poland 0 Portugal 1;
Portugal 1 Soviet Union 0

GROUP THREE	P	W	D	L	F	A	Pts
Denmark	8	6	1	1	17	5	13
England	8	5	2	1	23	3	12
Greece	8	3	2	3	8	10	8
Hungary	8	3	1	4	18	17	7
Luxembourg	8	0	0	8	5	36	0

Denmark 2 England 2; Luxembourg 0 Greece 2; Luxembourg 1
Denmark 2; Greece 0 England 3; England 9 Luxembourg 0;
Luxembourg 2 Hungary 6; England 0 Greece 0; Hungary 6
Luxembourg 2; England 2 Hungary 0; Denmark 1 Greece 0; Hungary 2
Greece 3; Denmark 3 Hungary 1; England 0 Denmark 1; Hungary 0
England 3; Denmark 6 Luxembourg 0; Hungary 1 Denmark 0; Greece 0
Denmark 2; Luxembourg 0 England 4; Greece 2 Hungary 2; Greece 1
Luxembourg 0

GROUP FOUR	P	W	D	L	F	A	Pts
Yugoslavia	6	3	2	1	12	11	8
Wales	6	2	3	1	7	6	7
Bulgaria	6	2	1	3	7	8	5
Norway	6	1	2	3	7	8	4

Wales 1 Norway 0; Norway 3 Yugoslavia 1; Bulgaria 2 Norway 2;
Bulgaria 0 Yugoslavia 1; Yugoslavia 4 Wales 4; Wales 1 Bulgaria 0;
Norway 1 Bulgaria 2; Norway 0 Wales 0; Yugoslavia 2 Norway 1;
Bulgaria 1 Wales 0; Wales 1 Yugoslavia 1; Yugoslavia 3 Bulgaria 2

GROUP FIVE	P	W	D	L	F	A	Pts
Romania	8	5	2	1	9	3	12
Sweden	8	5	1	2	14	5	11
Czech	8	3	4	1	15	7	10
Italy	8	1	3	4	6	12	5
Cyprus	8	0	2	6	4	21	2

Romania 3 Cyprus 1; Romania 2 Sweden 0; Czechoslovakia 2
Sweden 2; Italy 2 Czechoslovakia 2; Cyprus 0 Sweden 1; Italy 0
Romania 0; Cyprus 1 Italy 1; Cyprus 1 Czechoslovakia 1; Romania 1
Italy 0; Czechoslovakia 6 Cyprus 0; Sweden 5 Cyprus 0; Romania 0
Czechoslovakia 1; Sweden 2 Italy 0; Sweden 0 Romania 1; Sweden 1
Czechoslovakia 0; Italy 0 Sweden 3; Cyprus 0 Romania 1;
Czechoslovakia 2 Italy 0; Czechoslovakia 1 Romania 1; Italy 3 Cyprus 1

GROUP SIX	P	W	D	L	F	A	Pts
West Germany	8	5	1	2	15	5	11
Northern Ireland	8	5	1	2	8	5	11
Austria	8	4	1	3	15	10	9
Turkey	8	3	1	4	8	16	7
Albania	8	0	2	6	4	14	2

Austria 5 Albania 0; Austria 2 Northern Ireland 0; Turkey 1 Albania 0;
Northern Ireland 0; Austria 4 Turkey 0; Albania 0 Northern Ireland 0;
Northen Ireland 2 Turkey 1; Albania 1 West Germany 2; Turkey 0
West Germany 3; Austria 0 West Germany 0; Northern Ireland 1
Albania 0; Albania 1 Turkey 1; Albania 1 Austria 2; Northern Ireland 3
Austria 1; West Germany 3 Austria 0; Turkey 1 Northern Ireland 0;
West Germany 5 Turkey 1; West Germany 0 Northern Ireland 1; Turkey
3 Austria 1; West Germany 2 Albania 1

GROUP SEVEN	P	W	D	L	F	A	Pts
Spain	8	6	1	1	24	8	13
Holland	8	6	1	1	22	6	13
Republic of Ireland	8	4	1	3	20	10	9
Iceland	8	1	1	6	3	13	3
Malta	8	1	0	7	5	37	2

Malta 2 Iceland 1; Iceland 1 Holland 1; Holland 2 Republic of Ireland 1;
Republic of Ireland 2 Iceland 0; Spain 1 Iceland 0; Republic of Ireland 3
Spain 3; Malta 0 Holland 6; Spain 1 Holland 0; Malta 0
Republic of Ireland 1; Spain 2 Republic of Ireland 0; Malta 2 Spain 3;
Iceland 0 Spain 1; Iceland 1 Malta 0; Holland 3 Iceland 0; Iceland 0
Republic of Ireland 3; Republic of Ireland 2 Holland 3; Holland 2
Spain 1; Republic of Ireland 8 Malta 0; Holland 5 Malta 0; S
pain 12 Malta 1

France qualified as hosts

FINAL TOURNAMENT. 12-27 JUNE 1984

GROUP ONE	P	W	D	L	F	A	Pts
France	3	3	0	0	9	2	6
Denmark	3	2	0	1	8	3	4
Belgium	3	1	0	2	4	8	2
Yugoslavia	3	0	0	3	2	10	0

France 1 Denmark 0; Belgium 2 Yugoslavia 0; France 5 Belgium 0;
Denmark 5 Yugoslavia 0; France 3 Yugoslavia 2; Denmark 3 Belgium 2

GROUP TWO	P	W	D	L	F	A	Pts
Spain	3	1	2	0	3	2	4
Portugal	3	1	2	0	2	1	4
West Germany	3	1	1	1	2	2	3
Romania	3	0	1	2	2	4	1

Portugal 0 West Germany 0; Spain 1 Romania 1; West Germany 2
Romania 1; Portugal 1 Spain 1; Spain 1 West Germany 0; Portugal 1
Romania 0

SEMI-FINALS

France	3	–	2	Portugal (aet)
Spain	1	–	1	Denmark (5 - 4 pens)

FINAL Parc des Princes, Paris att: 47,000 27 June 1984

France	2	–	0	Spain

1988 A new generation of Dutch footballers won the eighth European Championship, held in West Germany. The outstanding trio of Van Basten, Gullit and Rijkaard were the stars of a team which played with a flexibility of formation, subtlety of movement and variation of attack that was reminiscent of their seventies predecessors who had been expected to win the World Cup fourteen years previously.

England, under the managment of Bobby Robson, who had led them to the quarter-finals of the 1986 World Cup, were one of the most impressive group winners of the qualifying rounds. Drawn in Group Four with Yugoslavia, Northern Ireland and Turkey, they got off to a confidence-boosting start against the Irish at Wembley in October 1986 with a 3-0 victory, Lineker continuing his international goalscoring form with two. A goalless draw away to Turkey was the only blemish on England's record, and they rounded off qualification in emphatic style with an 8-0 win over Turkey at Wembley and a systematic and skilful 4-1 defeat of Yugoslavia in Belgrade. The bitter memories of their failure to reach the 1984 finals had been erased, and with nineteen goals to one conceded and only one point dropped in six games, England were considered one of the favourites to lift the trophy.

Since his appointment in February 1986 as manager of the Republic of Ireland, Jack Charlton had instilled a tremendous team spirit and a belief in the system of play he had introduced. The direct, long-ball approach unsettled even the most technically gifted teams and the squad included some world-class players. The Irish were drawn alongside Scotland, Bulgaria, Belgium and Luxembourg in Group Seven, tough company from which to qualify for your first major international finals.

Scotland were also seeking their first qualification to the European Championship finals and started their campaign with a goalless draw at Hampden against Bulgaria. The Republic of Ireland earned a valuable point away to Belgium and played out a goalless draw against visitors Scotland before beating them 1-0 in the return leg.

Defeat at the hands of Bulgaria and a goalless draw at home to Belgium put a serious dent in the Republic of Ireland's chances, but they bounced back with victories over Luxembourg and were just a point behind leaders Bulgaria going into the next round, although they had played one game more. Scotland ended Belgium's slim hopes of qualification with a 2-0 win at Hampden and in the crucial game of the night, the Irish produced a rousing display to beat Bulgaria 2-0 in Dublin. A sad footnote to a magnificent performance was the dismissal of Brady, who struck Sadkov in the eighty-third minute in an evening fraught with intimidation.

Despite this setback, Bulgaria required only a draw at home against Scotland to secure qualification, but in the driving rain Mackay, making his international debut, darted through a defensive gap to score for the Scots. The Bulgarians had made the dangerous error of playing for the draw, and with little more than three minutes left they had no time to respond. Mackay was to receive a bumper postbag of Christmas cards from grateful Irish fans that year.

After getting themselves into a promising position with three good results at home – wins over Finland and Denmark and a 1-1 draw against Czechoslovakia – Wales' attempts to qualify from Group Six took a knock when they lost controversially to Denmark in Copenhagen. Elkjaer's fiftieth minute goal, despite a suspicion of offside, sent the Danes to the top of the table. Although the Welsh created enough chances to beat a lacklustre Czechoslovakia in their final game, Knoflicek's decisive thirty-first-minute goal, which also looked offside, ended their hopes. Bilek scored a second, which served only to rub salt in the wound.

Spain won five of their six Group One qualifying games to go through to the finals, but had a close call against Romania, who would have qualified themselves if they had beaten Austria in their final game.

After disappointing performances in the 1986 World Cup, the Italians, under new coach Azeglio Vicini, had started the process of rebuilding. Vicini had wasted little time drafting in members of the Under-21 side to complement more experienced players such as Baresi and Altobelli. Italy's priority was to develop a World Cup-winning team in time for 1990, when they would host the finals. In the process they comfortably overcame their Group Two qualifying opponents, Portugal, Sweden, Switzerland and Malta. Outstanding among the new players was Vialli, who scored two magnificent goals against Sweden, and in typical Italian style the frugal defence conceded only four goals in eight qualifying games.

Reigning champions France had reached the semi-finals of the

1986 World Cup, beating both Italy and Brazil along the way, but their qualification for the European Championship finals got off to a disastrous start with a goalless draw away to Group Four rivals Iceland. A 2-0 home reverse against the Soviet Union was followed by their only win, in the return match against Iceland. Another defeat, this time by Norway, effectively ended their hopes. Only East Germany appeared capable of preventing the Soviet Union progressing as group winners. The Germans took a first-half lead against them but the Soviets snatched a late equalizer and the point they required.

Holland were favourites in Group Five, which featured Greece, Poland and Cyprus, and justified their status by winning six of their games, conceding just one goal. The only obstacle to Holland's comfortable qualification was of their own, or rather of their fans', making. During the game against Cyprus in Rotterdam a smoke bomb was thrown from the crowd and hit the Cypriot goalkeeper. As he was carried off his team-mates refused to continue and were only reluctantly persuaded to return some time later. The Dutch won 8-0, but in view of the incident UEFA decided to award the game 3-0 to Cyprus. UEFA later settled on a replay behind closed doors, and although Cyprus held out for thirty-four minutes Holland eventually won by 4-0. The Cypriot goalkeeper, Pantziaras, held his own impromptu protest at UEFA's decision by refusing to retrieve the ball from his net after Koeman scored Holland's third goal from the penalty spot.

In spite of this controversy, the Dutch were certainly looking worthy contenders. Managed by Rinus Michels, the instigator of Dutch 'total football', the team were playing with the adventure and skill of Michels' 1974 World Cup finalists. And in Koeman, Rijkaard and Gullit, a world-record signing for Milan and European Footballer of the Year, Michels had three of the best players in world football. While Gullit received all the plaudits, he commented in an interview shortly before the finals that Van Basten, who had missed a number of games through injury, 'could be our greatest weapon. He has special ability to see goals and make space where there is none.' England and West Germany in particular ought to have paid more attention to his words.

The finals were held in West Germany. The hosts were drawn in Group One with Denmark, Italy and Spain while Group Two consisted of England, Holland, the Republic of Ireland and the Soviet Union. The action began on 10 June 1988 in Dusseldorf with West Germany against Italy, and the home side nearly conceded a goal within the first minute following Giannini's enterprising run. The tone of the first half was set as Italy continued to press forward warily and West Germany relied on counter-attacks. The deadlock was broken in the fifty-first minute when Donadoni capitalized on a misunderstanding between Matthäus and Herget to provide Mancini with his first international goal. Four minutes later the scores were level when the Italian goalkeeper, Zenga, was penalized for taking too many steps and Brehme's drive was deflected into the corner.

In Hanover the next day, Spain, well worth their 3-2 win over Denmark with goals from Michel, Butragueno and Gordillo, moved to the head of the group. West Germany needed a better performance than they had delivered against Italy to satisfy the home crowd, and four days later coach Franz Beckenbauer produced a much-improved display against Denmark: Klinsmann gave the Germans an early lead which they never looked like relinquishing, Thon headed in a second shortly before full-time and the hosts edged closer to the semi-finals.

Vialli squandered a hatful of chances before scoring the decider against Spain to put Italy back in contention. Spain now had the decidedly unenviable task of getting a result against the hosts who, after a shaky start, were gaining momentum as the competition progressed. West Germany's industrious midfielder Matthäus was a key figure in the game, and his control of the midfield was a major factor in establishing West German dominance. Voller put the Germans ahead after thirty minutes and added a second just after the restart.

Altobelli's and De Agostini's goals for Italy in their final game, against Denmark, put them level on points with West Germany but second in the table owing to a slightly inferior goal difference.

England's high hopes of success in the finals were brought tumbling down to earth after just five minutes of their opening game against the Republic of Ireland, supposedly the weakest team in the group. Sansom's sliced clearance was nodded on by Aldridge of Ireland to Houghton, who headed it into an obligingly large gap between Shilton and the far post. The Irish reinforced their defence and midfield, often leaving Aldridge as a lone striker, and their tight-knit organization held out against the English attack, which squandered a number of good chances. Bonner was magnificent in the Irish goal and the Irish dug in their heels to realize their ambition of conquering England for only the second time in their history.

In Cologne, the group received its second shock as the Soviet

Union, composed almost entirely of players from Dynamo Kiev, overcame the flamboyant skills of the Dutch with a second-half goal by Rats. Victory had seemed a formality for the Dutch, who dominated the play from the outset, and indeed Dasayev was forced into two brilliant first-half saves, from Koeman and Gullit, to keep the Soviets in the game. The Soviet Union, started the second half in more purposeful mood. The 1986 European Footballer of the Year, Belanov, forced a fine save from Van Breukelen and then supplied the pass which fell perfectly for Rats to score with a low drive.

The next game, between England and Holland, was crucial for both teams' chances and marked the first of three sensational performances from Van Basten, who had been out of action for a year following two ankle operations and had been a doubtful starter for the tournament. England started well and were unlucky not to be leading after both Lineker and Hoddle, with a curling free kick, hit the post. Just before half-time, the Dutch broke down the left and Gullit's low ball into the goalmouth was dragged away from Adams' lunging tackle by Van Basten and struck sweetly on the turn past Shilton. The half ended with Van Basten beating Shilton again, only for Stevens to clear from the line.

But within nine minutes of the second half England were level. Beardsley beat three Dutchmen and found Robson, who exchanged passes with Lineker before surging past two defenders and poking the ball past the goalkeeper. England deserved the goal but were undone in the seventy-second when Gullit put Van Basten through again after a free kick had been only half cleared. There is no substitute for incisive finishing, and Van Basten completed his hat-trick four minutes later, perfectly placed to thump in a flick-on from Koeman's corner. England were virtually out, but for the Dutch and Van Basten it was just the beginning.

In Hanover, the Republic of Ireland continued to confound their critics, this time with a deserved 1-1 draw against the Soviet Union. Whelan put the Irish ahead after thirty-eight minutes with as beautifully struck volley as one could hope to see from McCarthy's long throw, and there could have been more but for Dasayev's saves. But the Soviets' swift counter-attacks were always a danger, and with fifteen minutes left, Demyanenko's cross-field ball found Belanov, who slipped Protasov clear to beat Bonner.

England's final game ended in humiliation as they were swept aside by the Soviet Union who set the tone as early as the third minute with a goal by Aleinikov. By the time Adams equalized thirteen minutes later, the Soviet Union could have been out of sight as they had been carving through England's disorganized defence at will, only to squander their chances. The Soviets needed to win to guarantee a semi-final place. A mistake by Hoddle allowed Mikhailichenko to initiate and then finish a fluent move after twenty-six minutes to restore their lead, and although England played better in the second half, they could not stop Pasulko sweeping in for a third Soviet goal.

The fourth semi-final place was the prize on offer in the remaining game of the group and the Republic of Ireland came within eight minutes of continuing their fantastic run. They had defended defiantly for over eighty minutes and the Dutch were becoming increasingly desperate as they searched for the goal they needed to join the Soviet Union. When it came, it was a cruel blow for the underdogs. The Irish defence cleared the ball, but only as far as Koeman, whose drive bobbled up for Kieft to head it looping almost apologetically past the stranded Bonner.

In the first semi-final Holland met their old nemesis, West Germany, in Hamburg. The Germans suffered an early setback when their influential midfielder, Littbarski, was suddenly taken ill during the warm-up. Despite his absence the first half remained evenly balanced, although Van Basten and Gullit both came close to scoring. The Germans were forced to reorganize their resources again when Herget was injured in a collision with Gullit on half-time.

The game leaped into life nine minutes into the second half when West Germany were awarded a penalty after Rijkaard was judged, harshly, to have fouled Klinsmann. After a lengthy protest, Matthäus scored. Holland attempted to fashion a response and were steered back on course twenty minutes later when they were awarded a penalty for a similarly innocuous challenge, this time by Kohler on Van Basten. Koeman equalized. In an enthralling last quarter the Dutch pressed forward and were rewarded in the closing minutes when Wouters' marvellous pass was superbly struck home by Van Basten. It was a sweet victory for Holland, their first over West Germany since 1956, and one which went some way to erasing the bitter memories of the 1974 World Cup final. Apart from the timing of the goals, the games were strikingly similar: the eventual winners went behind, then equalized from the penalty spot, and then their top striker scored the winning goal.

The following day in Stuttgart the Soviet Union faced Italy in the second semi-final, although one could have been forgiven for thinking it was a game between Milan and Kiev, such was the reliance of both national teams on players from these clubs. The Soviet Union had combined great technical skill with a ruthless, physical approach to reach this stage and seven of their players carried yellow cards into the game. From the outset, they were determined to suppress the talent of the young Italian side, and in only the second minute, Kutznetzov, one of the seven 'card-carrying' players, was booked and thereby ruled himself out of a the final in the event that his side were successful.

In a ferocious game the Italians created the clearer opportunities, and had Vialli taken his chances before half-time the balance might have shifted. As it was, the Soviets took the lead on the hour when Kutznetzov played the ball to Litovchenko inside the area. He forced his way through several challenges before scoring. Three minutes later, Protasov made it two to leave Italy reflecting on what might have been. Still, it had been an important lesson in their preparations for the 1990 World Cup finals.

The final was played on 25 June in Munich's Olympic Stadium. Both teams had good reasons to be confident of success. The Soviet Union had already beaten Holland in the group stage, but the Dutch had got progressively better through the tournament and knew that Kutznetzov's absence from the Russian defence was crucial. The game started well with early chances for both teams: Koeman's howitzer of a free kick flew just over the bar and Litovchenko's shot was gratefully gathered by Van Breukelen.

In the thirty-third minute, the Dutch went ahead when Koeman's centre was nodded back square by Van Basten for Gullit to head past Dasayev. Belanov squandered a good opportunity to level the scores as the Soviet Union pressed forward, but in the fifty-fourth minute Van Basten showed just how a goal should be taken with an incredible shot from Muhren's far-post cross.

Van Breukelen needlessly gave away a penalty but then saved the kick from Belanov who was having something of a nightmare game, and although the Soviets never gave up, Holland were rarely troubled and could have extended their lead in the dying minutes.

So Holland had finally won their first major trophy, beaten their old rivals West Germany, and achieved both with style and flair.

QUALIFYING TOURNAMENT

GROUP ONE	P	W	D	L	F	A	Pts
Spain	6	5	0	1	14	6	10
Romania	6	4	1	1	13	3	9
Austria	6	2	1	3	6	9	5
Albania	6	0	0	6	2	17	0

Romania 4 Austria 0; Austria 3 Albania 0; Spain 1 Romania 0;
Albania 1 Spain 2; Romania 5 Albania 1; Austria 2 Spain 3; Albania 0
Austria 1; Romania 3 Spain 1; Spain 2 Austria 0; Albania 0 Romania 1;
Spain 5 Albania 0; Austria 0 Romania 0

GROUP TWO	P	W	D	L	F	A	Pts
Italy	8	6	1	1	16	4	13
Sweden	8	4	2	2	12	5	10
Portugal	8	2	4	2	6	8	8
Switzerland	8	1	5	2	9	9	7
Malta	8	0	2	6	4	21	2

Sweden 2 Switzerland 0; Portugal 1 Sweden 1; Switzerland 1
Portugal 1; Italy 3 Switzerland 2; Malta 0 Sweden 5; Malta 0 Italy 2;
Italy 5 Malta 0; Portugal 0 Italy 1; Portugal 2 Malta 2; Switzerland 4
Malta 1; Sweden 1 Malta 0; Sweden 1 Italy 0; Switzerland 1
Sweden 1; Sweden 0 Portugal 1; Switzerland 0 Italy 0; Portugal 0
Switzerland 0; Italy 2 Sweden 1; Malta 1 Switzerlnad 1; Italy 3
Portugal 0; Malta 0 Portugal 1

GROUP THREE	P	W	D	L	F	A	Pts
Soviet Union	8	5	3	0	14	3	13
East Germany	8	4	3	1	13	4	11
France	8	1	4	3	4	7	6
Iceland	8	2	2	4	4	14	6
Norway	8	1	2	5	5	12	4

Iceland 0 France 0; Iceland 1 Soviet Union 1; Norway 0 E. Germany 0;
France 0 Soviet Union 2; Soviet Union 4 Norway 0; E. Germany 2
Iceland 0; E. Germany 0 France 0; France 2 Iceland 0; Soviet Union 2
E. Germany 0; Norway 0 Soviet Union 1; Iceland 0 E. Germany 6;
Norway 2 France 0; Soviet Union 1 France 1; Iceland 2 Norway 1;
Norway 0 Iceland 1; E. Germany 1 Soviet Union 1; France 1 Norway 1;
Soviet Union 2 Iceland 0; E. Germany 3 Norway 1; France 0 E. Germany 1

GROUP FOUR	P	W	D	L	F	A	Pts
England	6	5	1	0	19	1	11
Yugoslavia	6	4	0	2	13	9	8
Northern Ireland	6	1	1	4	2	10	3
Turkey	6	0	2	4	2	16	2

England 3 Northern Ireland 0; Yugoslavia 4 Turkey 0; England 2
Yugoslavia 0; Turkey 0 Northern Ireland 0; Northern Ireland 0
England 2; Northern Ireland 1 Yugoslavia 2; Turkey 0 England 0;
Yugoslavia 3 Northen Ireland 0; England 8 Turkey 0; Yugoslavia 1
England 4; Northern Ireland 1 Turkey 0; Turkey 2 Yugoslavia 3

GROUP FIVE	P	W	D	L	F	A	Pts
Holland	8	6	2	0	15	1	14
Greece	8	4	1	3	12	13	9
Hungary	8	4	0	4	13	11	8
Poland	8	3	2	3	9	11	8
Cyprus	8	0	1	7	3	16	1

Hungary 0 Holland 1; Poland 2 Greece 1; Greece 2 Hungary 1;
Holland 0 Poland 0; Cyprus 2 Greece 4; Cyprus 0 Holland 2; Greece 3
Cyprus 1; Cyprus 0 Hungary 1; Holland 1 Greece 1; Poland 0 Cyprus 0;
Greece 1 Poland 0; Holland 2 Hungary 0; Hungary 5 Poland 3;
Poland 3 Hungary 2; Hungary 3 Greece 0; Poland 0 Holland 2;
Cyprus 0 Poland 1; Hungary 1 Cyprus 0; Greece 0 Holland 3;
Holland 4 Cyprus 0

GROUP SIX	P	W	D	L	F	A	Pts
Denmark	6	3	2	1	4	2	8
Czechoslovakia	6	2	3	1	7	5	7
Wales	6	2	2	2	7	5	6
Finland	6	1	1	4	4	10	3

Finland 1 Wales 1; Czechoslovakia 3 Finland 0; Denmark 1 Finland 0;
Czechoslovakia 0 Denmark 0; Wales 4 Finland 0; Finland 0 Denmark 1;
Wales 1 Czechoslovakia 1; Denmark 1 Czechoslovakia 1; Wales 1
Denmark 0; Finland 3 Czechoslovakia 0; Denmark 1 Wales 0;
Czechoslovakia 2 Wales 0

GROUP SEVEN	P	W	D	L	F	A	Pts
Republic of Ireland	8	4	3	1	10	5	11
Bulgaria	8	4	2	2	12	6	10
Belgium	8	3	3	2	16	8	9
Scotland	8	3	3	2	7	5	9
Luxembourg	8	0	1	7	2	23	1

Scotland 0 Bulgaria 0; Belgium 2 Republic of Ireland 2; Luxembourg 0
Belgium 6; Republic of Ireland 0 Scotland 0; Scotland 3 Luxembourg 0;
Belgium 1 Bulgaria 1; Scotland 0 Republic of Ireland 1; Bulgaria 2
Republic of Ireland 1; Belgium 4 Scotland 1; Republic of Ireland 0
Belgium 0; Luxembourg 1 Bulgaria 4; Bulgaria 3 Luxembourg 0;
Luxembourg 0 Republic of Ireland 2; Republic of Ireland 2
Luxembourg 1; Bulgaria 2 Belgium 0; Scotland 2 Belgium 0;
Republic of Ireland 2 Bulgaria 0; Belgium 3 Luxembourg 0;
Bulgaria 0 Scotland 1; Luxembourg 0 Scotland 0

West Germany qualified as hosts

FINAL TOURNAMENT. 10-25 JUNE 1988

GROUP ONE	P	W	D	L	F	A	Pts
West Germany	3	2	1	0	5	1	5
Italy	3	2	1	0	4	1	5
Spain	3	1	0	2	3	5	2
Denmark	3	0	0	3	2	7	0

West Germany 1 Italy 1; Spain 3 Denmark 2; West Germany 2 Denmark 0; Italy 1 Spain 0; West Germany 2 Spain 0; Italy 2 Denmark 0

GROUP TWO	P	W	D	L	F	A	Pts
Soviet Union	3	2	1	0	5	2	5
Holland	3	2	0	1	4	2	4
Republic of Ireland	3	1	1	1	2	2	3
England	3	0	0	3	2	7	0

Republic of Ireland 1 England 0; Soviet Union 1 Holland 0; Holland 3 England 1; Soviet Union 1 Republic of Ireland 1; Soviet Union 3 England 1; Holland 1 Republic of Ireland 0

SEMI-FINALS

West Germany	1	–	2	Holland
Soviet Union	2	–	0	Italy

FINAL Olympic Stadium, Munich att: 72,000 25 June 1988

Holland	2	–	0	Soviet Union

1992 In perhaps the most extraordinary chapter of European Championship history yet written Denmark were crowned European champions in Sweden after they had initially failed to qualify for the final stages. Many of the Danish players were on holiday when the team was invited to take the place of war-torn Yugoslavia a week before the tournament started. Not surprisingly, Denmark were not considered worthy challengers alongside the likes of Germany, Holland, England and France, but although they might not have had the best players in the competition, they proved that collectively they were the best-spirited and mentally the toughest team. The finals will not be remembered as a banquet of football excellence, but for drama, emotion and a double dose of giant-killing, it had no equal.

Having finished fourth in the 1990 World Cup under Bobby Robson, England approached the European Championship qualifiers with some degree of confidence. In truth, England had struggled against World Cup group rivals Egypt and had only squeaked past Belgium and Cameroon before losing to West Germany in a penalty shoot-out. But under new manager Graham Taylor they certainly looked as if they had the measure of their first challengers for the European Championship, Poland, Turkey and the Republic of Ireland in Group Seven.

England did indeed get off to a bright start, beating Poland 2-0 at Wembley, but this was to be their only convincing performance of the qualifiers. After a hollow 1-1 draw in Dublin, England were fortunate to hold on for the same result at Wembley where Jack Charlton's Ireland played superbly. The Irish dropped a vital point at home against Poland, but their disappointment turned to misery in the return game when they let slip a fine 3-1 lead in the final fifteen minutes to allow Poland to level the scores. That result meant that England required a point from their final game in Poznan if, as was expected, the Irish beat Turkey. Poland also had an outside chance of qualification and indeed they led against England until Lineker struck with just fourteen minutes left to secure the 1-1 draw England needed. After the game a very relieved Graham Taylor admitted he had been concerned. 'We missed three great chances and I was just hoping one would fall to Gary,' he said. 'Thankfully it did. The effort had all the hallmarks of the great goalscorer Gary is, and I'm delighted.'

Scotland finally made it through to their first-ever European Championship finals, topping a tight Group Two table from Switzerland, Romania, Bulgaria and San Marino. They got off to an excellent start, beating both Romania and Switzerland at Hampden, and maintained their unbeaten progress until they went down to a Hagi penalty in Bucharest. Having finished their own programme with a 4-0 home win against San Marino, the Scots were relying on Bulgaria to force a draw at home to Romania. Popescu put the Romanians ahead after twenty-nine minutes and when Mikhailov brought down Rotariouiou in the penalty area Scottish hopes took another tumble. But Hagi's spot-kick was saved, and ten minutes into the second half Sirakov equalized for Bulgaria to put Scotland through.

Wales' hopes of joining England and Scotland were dealt a severe blow when they were drawn against world champions Germany, with Belgium and Luxembourg making up Group Five. However, Germany are often not the best of starters and indeed they made hard work of beating Luxembourg 3-2 away and Belgium 1-0 at home. In their opening games, Wales narrowly beat Luxembourg and then took a point in Belgium before facing Germany in Cardiff. Southall produced a series of fine saves to keep the Germans at bay, but the game took on a different perspective when Berthold was sent off, forcing the Germans to reorganize their defence. Rush exploited the situation by lashing the ball past Illgner to give Wales a famous victory.

Typically, German manager Berti Vogts transformed the team for the return and Wales suffered a fierce onslaught as they were beaten 4-1. Germany were now into their stride and ensured qualification with victories over Belgium and Luxembourg.

There were no hiccups in France's qualification. Under the inspirational leadership of new coach Michel Platini, they were alone in winning all their matches in a group which included Spain and Czechoslovakia. Platini, like Franz Beckenbauer, had proved that previous experience was not a prerequisite for success as an international manager and had instilled commitment and resilience into a team which already possessed the traditional Gallic qualities. And in Papin the French had an outstanding striker who was potentially a championship winner.

Reigning European champions Holland restored Rinus Michels as manager after their disastrous showing in the 1990 World Cup, but they had their problems in the early stages. Many players had favoured the appointment of Johan Cruyff rather than Michels and amid these internal wranglings Rijkaard announced his retirement from international football and Koeman was discarded by Michels after publicly criticizing his team's tactics in a friendly with Italy. Against this backdrop of dissension, their 1-0 defeat in Portugal was almost inevitable.

Problems continued when Gullit pulled out of their second game against Greece, but Van Basten and his exciting new striking partner, Bergkamp, both scored in a 2-0 win. The turning point for Holland came six days before Christmas, when they thrashed Malta 8-0, Van Basten scoring five, a tally which dramatically improved their goal difference. Their crucial game was in mid-October 1991, when Holland entertained Portugal in Rotterdam. Rijkaard's decision to come out of retirement was a welcome boost and Witschge's goal put the Dutch back on course. Greece still had an outside chance but Holland beat them in Athens despite the loss of Gullit with a pulled muscle sustained in the warm-up.

But if the Dutch felt they had problems they were nothing compared to those occupying the minds of players from the Soviet Union and Yugoslavia. In September 1991 the three Baltic States of Lithuania, Latvia and Estonia gained independence from the Soviet Union and the remaining twelve republics quickly followed suit. Despite all the upheavals, the Commonwealth of Independent States, or CIS, as it came to be called, held off their Group Three challengers, which included Italy, to book their place in the finals.

Yugoslavia had long been one of the world's most stylish footballing nations, producing a steady stream of world-class players. They had often failed to win the ultimate prize in international competitions, despite frequent displays of superior skill and technique, but the national squad that started in the 1992 European Championship qualifiers proved themselves to be an exceptionally talented team. In 1991, old nationalist tensions resurfaced in Yugoslavia and the country disintegrated into a bloody and violent civil war. The fighting between Serbs and Croats deprived the national side of all their Croatian stars. Yet Yugoslavia still won their group, scoring twenty-four goals, conceding just four, with Pancev and Savicevic outstanding.

In the build-up to the finals, Yugoslavia played Holland in a friendly in March 1992. Shortly afterwards they were banned from the competition as part of the sanctions imposed on their country.

Denmark, who had finished second in their group were invited at short notice to take their place.

The hosts, Sweden, went into the finals as something of an unknown quantity. The friendly matches they had played in preparation for the tournament gave little indication of their ability: good performances such as a 4-0 win over Denmark were followed by poor ones, but Thern and Schwarz looked commanding in midfield and Brolin was forming an impressive understanding with the pacy Dahlin in attack.

Sweden were drawn in Group One with France, England and Denmark, while Group Two consisted of Germany, Holland, Scotland and the CIS.

Sweden opened the finals on 10 June against France and rose to the occasion with a sterling display. They deservedly took the lead after twenty-four minutes when Eriksson headed home from Limpar's corner kick and continued to pressurize the French defence throughout the first half. Papin had a justifiable claim for a penalty turned down, but it wasn't until the second half and the introduction of Perez for Vahirua that France began to look dangerous. In the fifty-eighth minute, Papin met Perez's angled cross to beat Ravelli with his only significant contribution of the afternoon. Ingesson hit the post with a powerful header, but the French defence were getting to grips with the Swedish attack and in the end both teams seemed happy with the draw.

The following day injury-ravaged England met newly arrived Denmark. England had lost Barnes, Stevens (himself a replacement for Jones and Dixon) and Liverpool's Wright in quick succession and in the circumstances did well to shade the first half. In the second half the Danes began to move the ball more fluently and Jensen in particular began to stretch England. He came closest to breaking the deadlock with an angled shot that hit the post, but honours remained even at the final whistle.

England's second match, against France in Malmö, was marred by hooligan trouble in the city centre the night before. Trouble had flared when riot police with horses and dogs were called in after a few youths decided to climb on top of a beer tent and the resulting confrontation left a number of people requiring hospital treatment. The game itself ended in another bore-draw totally lacking in any entertainment value. Graham Taylor brought in Shearer alongside

Lineker and the partnership created a few chances, but it was Pearce who almost put England on the scoreboard eight minutes from time. Having had the blood wiped from his face following a clash of heads with Boli, Pearce promptly ran back on to the pitch to fire a ferocious free kick against the bar.

In the group's other game that day, Sweden made just one change from the team that had begun against France, replacing Andersson with the more mobile Dahlin, and attacked the Danes from the very start. Dahlin combined well with Brolin and caused problems in the Danish defence as Thern, Schwarz and Limpar created good openings. After half an hour, Denmark belatedly got into the game as Vilfort went close and Christofte's powerful free kick forced a fine save from Ravelli. The Danes maintained their attacking momentum at the start of the second half, but the decisive strike came from Sweden. Thern played a delightful ball to Dahlin, who beat Nielsen before crossing the ball into the centre. Olsen cleared it from the advancing Schwarz, but only into the path of Brolin, who scored. In an entertaining finale, both teams had further chances but when the whistle went Sweden had clinched both points and headed the group.

England needed to win their final group game against Sweden to get through to the semi-finals and Graham Taylor made yet further changes in his effort to find a winning formation. His decision to push Platt forward to partner Lineker was almost magically vindicated when he scored from Lineker's cross after only three minutes. England were unrecognizable from their previous matches. The defence looked solid against the twin threat of Brolin and Dahlin and as the half ended England looked more likely to extend their lead than the Swedes did to regain the lost ground.

For the second half, Swedish manager Tommy Svensson introduced Ekstrom to support his two strikers and his presence made all the difference when, in the fifty-first minute, Eriksson headed his side level from a corner. Swedish confidence blossomed as they increased the pressure on an England side which was losing shape. Eriksson headed another corner kick against the bar as the Swedes continued to beat England at their own game. In a desperate last bid, Taylor replaced Lineker with Smith in the sixty-second minute but Sweden were now dominating the game and scored a magnificent winner twenty minutes later. Brolin picked up the ball in midfield and played a one-two first with Ingesson, then with Dahlin, as he accelerated through the English defence and slotted the ball past Woods.

It was a sad exit for England and for Gary Lineker in his last international. Taylor claimed that his team needed someone who could hold the ball up, which wasn't Lineker's style but it could also be argued that what England needed was the presence of the one man whose record had proved him capable of snatching the one chance that might arise.

Going into their game against France, Denmark were so unfancied that bookmakers were offering 80-1 against them winning the championship. They had also lost the services of Vilfort, who had returned home as concern mounted about the condition of his daughter, who was being treated for leukaemia. His place went to Larsen, who struck a fine first goal just seven minutes into the game. France had performed well below their potential in their previous matches and even now, on the verge of an ignominious exit from the finals, they failed to raise their game beyond the physically robust. That they got back into the game at all was due to another flash of brilliance from Papin, who beat Schmeichel in the sixtieth minute with a powerful, precise shot from his only chance in the game. Denmark's coach, Richard Moller Nielsen, sent on Elstrup in what turned out to be another inspirational decision: he scored from Povlsen's cross with just twelve minutes remaining.

In Group Two, Holland dominated the first half of their game against Scotland with Gullit, in particular, in superb form. Scotland, however, refused to be overwhelmed and put together several attacking flurries of their own in the second half, only for Gullit to initiate a rapid passing movement with Rijkaard and Van Basten which allowed Bergkamp to score from the edge of the 6-yard box.

Germany faced the CIS on the same day and were tactically outsmarted by their renamed opponents. The talent of the CIS players was undisputed, but a question-mark hung over the team spirit among players who would soon be playing for different countries. In the event, Germany's almost relentless first-half pressure was weathered by the CIS, whose tactic of playing without a central striker effectively cut the Geman sweeper, Binz, out of the game. After just over an hour's play, Dobrovolski was bundled over by Reuter in the penalty area and the winger got up to put the CIS ahead. Seeing the game slipping away, Vogts brought on Klinsmann and Germany threw everything at levelling the score. In the last minute, they were awarded a free kick on the edge of the area and Hassler curled his shot into the net.

Having survived this scare against the CIS, Germany regained their winning ways against Scotland in an excellent game. The Scots attacked from the start and Illgner made vital saves from Gough, McAllister and McClair within the opening fifteen minutes. Klinsmann had been installed as replacement for the injured Voller, and played a decisive role in setting up the ball for Riedle to rifle a shot past Goram in the twenty-ninth minute. Effenberg extended the lead less than two minutes into the second half when his cross was deflected in a crazy loop over Goram's head, but Scotland never gave in and took the game to Germany. Moller and Hassler saw their shots rebound off the Scottish post, but head injuries to Reuter and Buchwald must have left Germany relieved to hear the final whistle.

For their second game Holland stuck with the side that had beaten Scotland, but against a well-organized CIS they struggled to create sufficient clear-cut openings. When they did find a way through, Kharin in the CIS goal was equal to the task, making a series of courageous and acrobatic saves. In addition Van Basten had a good goal ruled offside, and the game ended 0-0, with both teams still in with a chance of progressing.

The Dutch marched through to the semi-finals with a brilliant and sweet victory over an injury-hit Germany, who were worst affected in defence because of the head injuries to Reuter and Buchwald. It took Holland just two minutes to breach the reorganized defence as Rijkaard headed past Illgner. Witschge drove home a free kick in the fourteenth minute to make it two and Van Basten hit the bar with a cracking volley: Germany were suffering in a way they had seldom suffered before. They were not in the same game. Their only consolation at half-time was that Scotland were leading the CIS, which meant they could still qualify.

Vogts brought on Sammer for the more defensive Helmer in the second half and German fortunes changed when Klinsmann headed home a corner in the fifty-third minute to reduce the deficit. But Bergkamp re-established Holland's two-goal lead with a header from Winter's well-judged cross.

Germany qualified for the semis thanks to Scotland's decisive 3-0 victory over the CIS, who had proved such problematic opponents to both Germany and Holland. Scotland took the lead after only six minutes, McStay driving his shot through a pack of defenders, and ten minutes later McClair scored the first goal for his country to put them 2-0 up. The CIS dominated much of the first half but lacked the penetration to finish off their sweet passing moves. McAllister scored Scotland's third shortly before time from the penalty spot after Nevin had been tripped up.

In the first semi-final, Germany faced Sweden in Stockholm. While Germany welcomed the return of Buchwald and Reuter, Sweden were without Andersson and, more importantly, Schwarz from midfield. A Hassler special put Germany ahead in the tenth minute when he placed his free kick through the edge of the wall and down past Ravelli's right hand. Sammer should have scored a second and Brehme rattled the crossbar after a tapped free kick from Hassler as Germany continued to dominate the first half.

After the interval, Riedle put Germany further ahead in the fifty-eighth minute following good approach work by Hassler. But Sweden were offered a lifeline when Ingesson went crashing down in the penalty area following Helmer's challenge. Brolin converted the spot-kick for his third of the tournament. Riedle restored Gemany's advantage in the eighty-eighth minute after Helmer had presented him with an easy opportunity, and although Sweden hit back immediately from the kick-off with a header from Andersson, they seemed to lack the total conviction they had shown against England and never appeared to believe they could win the game. As for Germany, they were through to yet another major final.

The following day, Holland faced the championship's unlikely heroes, Denmark, who welcomed the returning Vilfort back into their midfield. Any preconceived ideas the Dutch may have harboured that this would be an easy ride were dispelled within five minutes as Laudrup's cross was headed home by Larsen. Holland went on the offensive, but it was not until the twenty-third minute that they got back into the game when Bergkamp struck his third goal of the tournament following an excellent move. Dutch relief was short-lived. Denmark regained the lead in the thirty-second minute with a second goal for Larsen.

The Dutch spent almost all of the second half on the attack and although the Danes looked dangerous on the break they lost Laudrup and Andersen through injury and the hobbling Sivebaek was moved into attack. It was only going to be a matter of time before Holland scored, yet Denmark hung on until five minutes from time, when Rijkaard stabbed home the equalizer to send the tie into extra time. Holland had left it very late, but surely they only had to stay on their feet to beat the exhausted Danes. Schmeichel kept Denmark on level terms with several fine saves in extra time and the game moved on to the penalty shoot-out.

Ironically, it was Van Basten, regarded as the best finisher in the world, who saw his effort parried by Schmeichel and as each Danish player converted his spot-kick it was left to Christofte to calmly put home the decisive penalty which sent Denmark into the final.

Denmark had arrived in Sweden with nothing to prove and now they were in the final. The gruelling semi-final had left the team exhausted and none who saw them hobbling off the pitch after that game could seriously believe they would be able to raise their game against Germany, who had the additional benefit of an extra day's rest.

On 26 June, the Ullevi Stadium was awash with red and white as the Danish fans did their utmost to lift their heroes. However, the opening exchanges were dominated by the Germans as Reuter and Klinsmann both went close. Suddenly, Denmark started to string their passes together and took the lead after eighteen minutes. Vilfort dispossessed Brehme and set Polvsen free on the right. He beat his man before pulling the ball back for Jensen to strike a glorious drive past Illgner from the edge of the area. Within minutes Schmeichel pushed away another low shot from Klinsmann, but a rash of bad tackles spoiled the continuity of the game as first Piechnik, for Denmark, and then Effenberg and Hassler of Germany were booked. Hassler was marked so well by Christofte that the tournament's best player could not influence proceedings as he had done in previous matches and Germany were less dangerous as a result.

Germany had the better of the second half, too, as they looked for the equalizer. Nielsen cleared Klinsmann's far-post cross acrobatically off the line and from the resulting corner Schmeichel brilliantly tipped the German striker's flying header over the bar. Vilfort had squandered a chance in the seventy-first minute to put Denmark two up, but he made no mistake seven minutes later. Yet there was an element of fortune to the goal. Germany failed to clear a free kick effectively and Christiansen headed the ball to Vilfort who appeared to have brushed the ball with his forearm before bursting through to shoot powerfully past Illgner. But German protests were dismissed by the referee. For once the Germans' famed powers of recovery were not forthcoming, and Denmark held on for the remainder of the game to achieve the greatest victory in their footballing history.

Nobody could begrudge Denmark their victory. How they had kept running in extra time against Holland had been nothing short of a miracle, but they had succeeded by putting a premium on teamwork and had supported each other tirelessly with wonderful displays of defence and counter-attack. Their amiable manager, Richard Moller Nielsen, who had planned to decorate his kitchen during the weeks of the championship, vowed before each game that his players would give everything they had. 'I don't promise that we will win,' he had kept saying. 'But we will try our hardest to win.' That, in the end, was more than enough.

QUALIFYING TOURNAMENT

GROUP ONE	P	W	D	L	F	A	Pts
France	8	8	0	0	20	6	16
Czechoslovakia	8	5	0	3	12	9	10
Spain	7	3	0	4	17	12	6
Iceland	8	2	0	6	7	10	4
Albania	7	1	0	6	2	21	2

Iceland 2 Albania 0; Iceland 1 France 2; Czechoslovakia 1 Iceland 0; Spain 2 Iceland 1; France 2 Czechoslovakia 1; Czechoslovakia 3 Spain 2; Albania 0 France 1; Spain 9 Albania 0; France 3 Spain 1; France 5 Albania 0; Albania 0 Czechoslovkia 2; Albania 1 Iceland 0; Iceland 0 Czechoslovkia 1; Czechoslovkia 1 France 2; Iceland 2 Spain 0; Spain 1 France 2; Czechoslovkia 2 Albania 1; Spain 2 Czechoslovkia 1; France 3 Iceland 1; Albania v Spain not played

GROUP TWO	P	W	D	L	F	A	Pts
Scotland	8	4	3	1	14	7	11
Switzerland	8	4	2	2	19	7	10
Romania	8	4	2	2	13	7	10
Bulgaria	8	3	3	2	15	8	9
San Marino	8	0	0	8	1	33	0

Switzerland 2 Bulgaria 0; Scotland 2 Romania 1; Romania 0 Bulgaria 3;
Scotland 2 Switzerland 1; Bulgaria 1 Scotland 1; San Marino 0
Switzerland 4; Romania 6 San Marino 0; Scotland 1 Bulgaria 1;
San Marino 1 Romania 3; Switzerland 0 Romania 0; Bulgaria 2
Switzerland 3; San Marino 0 Scotland 2; San Marino 0 Bulgaria 3;
Switzerland 7 San Marino 0; Switzerland 2 Scotland 2; Bulgaria 4
San Marino 0; Romania 1 Scotland 0; Scotland 4 San Marino 0;
Romania 1 Switzerland 0; Bulgaria 1 Romania 1

GROUP THREE	P	W	D	L	F	A	Pts
CIS	8	5	3	0	13	2	13
Italy	8	3	4	1	12	5	10
Norway	8	3	3	2	9	5	9
Hungary	8	2	4	2	10	9	8
Cyprus	8	0	0	8	2	25	0

CIS 2 Norway 0; Norway 0 Hungary 0; Hungary 1 Italy 1; Hungary 4
Cyprus 2; Italy 0 CIS 0; Cyprus 0 Norway 3; Cyprus 0 Italy 4; Cyprus 0
Hungary 2; Hungary 0 CIS 1; Italy 3 Hungary 1; Norway 3 Cyprus 0;
CIS 4 Cyprus 0; Norway 2 Italy 1; Norway 0 CIS 1; CIS 2 Hungary 2;
CIS 0 Italy 0; Hungary 0 Norway 0; Italy 1 Norway 1; Cyprus 0 CIS 3;
Italy 2 CIS 0;

GROUP FOUR	P	W	D	L	F	A	Pts
Yugoslavia	8	7	0	1	24	4	14
Denmark	8	6	1	1	18	7	13
Northern Ireland	8	2	3	3	11	11	7
Austria	8	1	1	6	6	14	3
Faroe Islands	8	1	1	6	3	26	3

Northern Ireland 0 Yugoslavia 2; Faroe Islands 1 Austria 0; Denmark 4
Faroe Islands 1; Northern Ireland 1 Denmark 1; Yugoslavia 4 Austria 1;
Denmark 0 Yugoslavia 2; Austria 0 Northern Ireland 0; Yugoslavia 4
Northern Ireland 1; Yugoslavia 1 Denmark 2; Northern Ireland 1
Faroe Islands 1; Yugoslavia 7 Faroe Islands 0; Austria 3 Faroe Islands 0;

Denmark 2 Austria 1; Faroe Islands 0 Northern Ireland 5; Faroe Islands 0
Denmark 4; Austria 0 Denmark 3; Faroe Islands 0 Yugoslavia 2;
Northern Ireland 2 Austria 1; Denmark 2 Northern Ireland 1;
Austria 0 Yugoslavia 2

GROUP FIVE	P	W	D	L	F	A	Pts
Germany	6	5	0	1	13	4	10
Wales	6	4	1	1	8	6	9
Belgium	6	2	1	3	7	6	5
Luxembourg	6	0	0	6	2	14	0

Wales 3 Belgium 1; Luxembourg 2 Germany 3; Luxembourg 0 Wales 1;
Belgium 3 Luxembourg 0; Belgium 1 Wales 1; Germany 1 Belgium 0;
Wales 1 Germany 0; Luxembourg 0 Belgium 2; Germany 4 Wales 1;
Wales 1 Luxembourg 0; Belgium 0 Germany 1; Germany 4 Luxembourg 0

GROUP SIX	P	W	D	L	F	A	Pts
Holland	8	6	1	1	17	2	13
Portugal	8	5	1	2	11	4	11
Greece	8	3	2	3	11	9	8
Finland	8	1	4	3	5	8	6
Malta	8	0	2	6	2	23	2

Finland 0 Portugal 0; Portugal 1 Holland 0; Greece 4 Malta 0; Holland 2
Greece 0; Malta 1 Finland 1; Malta 0 Holland 8; Greece 3 Portugal 2;
Malta 0 Portugal 1; Portugal 5 Malta 0; Holland 1 Malta 0; Holland 2
Finland 0; Finland 2 Malta 0; Finland 1 Holland 1; Portugal 1 Finland 0;
Finland 1 Greece 1; Holland 1 Portugal 0; Greece 2 Finland 0;
Portugal 1 Greece 0; Greece 0 Holland 2; Malta 1 Greece 1

GROUP SEVEN	P	W	D	L	F	A	Pts
England	6	3	3	0	7	3	9
Republic of Ireland	6	2	4	0	13	6	8
Poland	6	2	3	1	8	6	7
Turkey	6	0	0	6	1	14	0

England 2 Poland 0; Republic of Ireland 5 Turkey 0; Republic of Ireland 1
England 1; Turkey 0 Poland 1; England 1 Republic of Ireland 1; Poland 3
Turkey 0; Turkey 0 England 1; Republic of Ireland 0 Poland 0; Poland 3
Republic of Ireland 3; England 1 Turkey 0; Poland 1 England 1; Turkey 1
Republic of Ireland 3

Sweden qualified as hosts. Denmark replaced Yugoslavia

FINAL TOURNAMENT. 10-26 JUNE 1992

GROUP ONE	P	W	D	L	F	A	Pts
Sweden	3	2	1	0	4	2	5
Denmark	3	1	1	1	2	2	3
France	3	0	2	1	2	3	2
England	3	0	2	1	1	2	2

Sweden 1 France 1; Denmark 0 England 0; France 0 England 0;
Sweden 1 Denmark 0; Sweden 2 England 1; Denmark 2 France 1

GROUP TWO	P	W	D	L	F	A	Pts
Holland	3	2	1	0	4	1	5
Germany	3	1	1	1	4	4	3
Scotland	3	1	0	2	3	3	2
CIS	3	0	2	1	1	4	2

Holland 1 Scotland 0; Germany 1 CIS 1; Germany 2 Scotland 0;
Holland 0 CIS 0; Scotland 3 CIS 0; Holland 3 Germany 1

SEMI-FINALS

Germany	3 – 2	Sweden
Denmark	2 – 2	Holland (5-4 pens)

FINAL Ullevi Stadium att: 37,000 26 June 1992

Denmark	2 – 0	Germany

THE ALL-TIME EUROPEAN CHAMPIONSHIP GREATS

Who is the greatest ever? Who's to say? Well we all are. Admittedly, it's virtually impossible to compare players from one generation to the next but that has never stopped anyone from whiling away endless hours discussing the merits of his or her own particular favourites. The word 'great' is grossly overused and has been applied to thousands of players so in compiling this greatest European Championship team we have imposed a few rules of eligibility. First, the player must have competed in the championship finals, so that rules out George Best for a start. And secondly, the player must have been in such inspirational form that he played a major part in the championship. We'd have to leave out the likes of Eusebio on this point. Other than that it could be anyone. The chances are that a collection of such brilliant individuals wouldn't work together as a team, but it would certainly be worth paying a lot of money to see them try.

LEV YASHIN
Goalkeeper: **Soviet Union, 1960**

No surprises here but it was a close call between Yashin and Ivo Viktor, whose heroic performances against West Germany in the 1976 final were instrumental in Czechoslovakia surviving extra time and then winning the penalty shoot-out. After due consideration, we have to elect Yashin as the best goalkeeper ever, and he takes the accolade if only because he wore black before Viktor did. Big, brave and athletic, he saved shots he had no business getting close to, never mind reaching. Those skills were on display in the final of the inaugural championship when Yugoslavia threatened to overrun the Soviet Union. Yashin responded with a series of fine saves to keep his team in the game, which they finally went on to win 2-1. The Soviet team was good but not great: the difference was that they had Yashin.

ERIC GERETS
Full-back: **Belgium, 1980**

The bearded Belgian was one of the leading players in the side that performed so well in the early eighties. He was the backbone supporting the rest of the defence and first came to the attention of a worldwide audience in the 1980 finals. His solid and consistent displays on the right side of defence helped Belgium reach the final where they lost to a last-minute goal from Hrubesch. The Germans had been expected to win the game easily. Gerets made sure they didn't.

GIACINTO FACCHETTI
Full-back: **Italy, 1968**

It may not come as a surprise to find an Italian player occupying one of the full-back positions, but Facchetti was not from the stopper school of, say, Claudio Gentile. He started his career as a centre forward and it wasn't until he signed for Inter that he moved to full-back, from where he would stride purposefully upfield in support of his forwards. He was a key figure in the formidable Italian team which won the 1968 European Championship and was one of the few full-backs who was effective at making use of the freedom created by the *catennaccio* system at Inter. He timed his tackles to perfection and seldom suffered the indignity of being beaten.

FRANK RIJKAARD
Defender: **Holland, 1988**

Rijkaard played in midfield for Milan but usually in central defence for Holland, which is where he would slot in here, alongside Beckenbauer. Such was the fluid nature of the Dutch side that won in 1988 that Rijkaard was able to operate as an all-purpose player. Quick and tough-tackling in defence, he had the awareness and technique to set up the attack.

FRANZ BECKENBAUER
Sweeper: **West Germany, 1972-76**

Probably the first name on the list. Beckenbauer started his career in midfield but it is in the revolutionary role of the attacking sweeper, which he created at Bayern Munich, that he is included here. It is almost an insult to refer to him as a mere defender, such was the accuracy of his passing and vision for initiating attacks. An elegant player, Beckenbauer was always in control and possessed the technique, athleticism and confidence to carry the ball through and beyond midfield. Take your pick from any of his performances in either the 1972 or 1976 European Championship finals.

GUNTHER NETZER
Midfielder: **West Germany, 1972**

Netzer was never one of football's workers, but his superb technique, speed and ability at dead-ball situations combined to make him an inspirational player and the epitome of West Germany's new era of total football. He was at his very best in the 1972 European Championship-winning side where his skill and vision in midfield were the perfect complement to the insatiable appetite for goals of Beckenbauer and Müller. The only downside was a clash of personalities between Netzer and Beckenbauer, which was never better illustrated than during a game against Norway before the 1972 finals. West Germany were awarded a free kick and Netzer, famous for scoring from such positions, took the ball, cleaned it, placed it and stepped back only for Beckenbauer to run up, shoot and score. We'd have to take the risk that this wouldn't have a detrimental effect on the team spirit of our side.

JOHAN NEESKENS
Midfielder: **Holland, 1976**

Neeskens was a superlative midfield dynamo who provided the steel in the great Dutch side of the 1970s and would ensure that the midfield of our select team possessed a tough yet talented element. He was a fierce, hard-tackling midfielder who fitted perfectly into the total-football philosophy of Ajax and Holland and it was these attributes which complemented the more technical skills of teammates such as Cruyff. Endlessly energetic, Neeskens also scored plenty of goals with powerful, thumping drives, or through bravely getting on to the end of balls played into the penalty area.

MICHEL PLATINI
Midfielder: **France, 1984**

The French national team of the 1980s was one of the most artistic and talented sides ever to have graced the international stage. In the 1984 European Championship the side included one of the best midfield line-ups ever of Jean Tigana, Alain Giresse, Luís Fernandez and, of course, Michel Platini, who more than anyone exemplified the true artistry and flair of French football. His individual skill and inspirational captaincy in that championship guarantees him a place in the Select XI midfield. His performances in those finals elevated him to share the status enjoyed by players like Pele, Cruyff and Beckenbauer. He scored nine goals in the five games, including two dazzling hat-tricks against Belgium and Yugoslavia respectively and one of his speciality curling free kicks in the final against Spain.

JOHAN CRUYFF
Striker: **Holland, 1976**

Although the European Championship ws not the stage for Cruyff's finest moments, he was still a major factor in Holland's achievement of reaching the semi-finals in 1976. Anyway, it would be impossible to leave one of the world's greatest all-round players out of this team. Cruyff's acceleration over 10 metres left the quickest defenders for dead and his control and passing ability at speed were unsurpassed. He would roam from midfield to the wings and then pop up as a nominal centre forward and defences would find it practically impossible to pick him up.

GERD MÜLLER
Striker: **West Germany, 1972**

Gerd Müller was a striker with an instinct for scoring goals. They may not have been spectacular strikes from 25 yards, but once he was inside the penalty area he always seemed to be quickest to react to the half-chance, quickest to the ball, and lethal in his execution. He would spend hours in practice making darting runs and quick turns, confident that he could turn faster than big defenders. His goalscoring record for club and country was phenomenal: sixty-eight goals in sixty-two internationals, 365 goals in the Bundesliga and thirty-six in the European Cup. He scored eleven goals in the 1972 European Championship campaign, two of them in the semi-final against Belgium and another two in the 3-0 win over the Soviet Union in the final. He was not the most elegant striker in Europe but probably the most effective.

MARCO VAN BASTEN
Striker: **Holland, 1988**

An all-round striker who could score with his head and both feet as well as create chances for others. Van Basten had been troubled with injury before the 1988 European Championship finals and was only a substitute in Holland's first game, but against England he scored as clinical a hat-trick as you could wish to see and once he got into his stride there was nothing to stop him from dominating the tournament. He left it until the final minute before scoring another splendidly taken goal to beat Germany in the semi-final and capped his performance in the final with one of the all-time great goals when he volleyed Mühren's high cross over a statuesque Dasayev. After five ankle operations, the thirty-year-old star has finally been forced to concede defeat to the injury which sidelined him for three seasons. It has put an untimely end to the career of one of the all-time great strikers.

EURO '96 DREAM TEAM

4-3-3

LEV YASHIN

ERIC GERETS   GIACINTO FACHETTI

FRANK RIJKAARD   FRANZ BECKENBAUER

JOHAN NEESKENS   GUNTHER NETZER   MICHEL PLATINI

JOHAN CRUYFF   GERD MULLER   MARCO VAN BASTEN

FIXTURE GUIDE

There's no getting away from it – you'll be spending the next three weeks in front of the television. So that you don't miss any vital game, and to help you make the best of any 'free' time, here's a useful day-by-day fixture guide to the championship. The BBC will have first choice of the quarter-finals when the competition reaches the knock-out phase but if either England or Scotland reach the semi-finals, it is probable that both BBC and ITV will provide coverage.

GROUP MATCHES	Winners
Saturday 8 June	
Group A: **England v Switzerland** (Wembley, 3.00 pm) ITV	1–1
Sunday 9 June	
Group B: **Spain v Bulgaria** (Elland Road, 2.30 pm) ITV	
Group C: **Germany v Czech Republic** (Old Trafford, 5.00 pm) BBC	2–0
Group D: **Denmark v Portugal** (Hillsborough, 7.30 pm) BBC	

Monday 10 June
Group A: **Holland v Scotland**   0–0
(Villa Park, 4.30 pm) ITV

Group B: **Romania v France**   1 0
(St James' Park, 7.30 pm) BBC

Tuesday 11 June
Group C: **Italy v Russia**   2–1
(Anfield, 4.30 pm) BBC

Group D: **Turkey v Croatia**   0–1
(City Ground, 7.30 pm) ITV

Wednesday 12 June
First free day. Replenish provisions.

Thursday 13 June
Group B: **Bulgaria v Romania**
(St James' Park, 4.30 pm) ITV

Group A: **Switzerland v Holland**
(Villa Park, 7.30 pm) BBC

Friday 14 June
Group D: **Portugal v Turkey**
(City Ground, 4.30 pm) BBC

Group C: **Czech Republic v Italy**
(Anfield, 7.30 pm) ITV

Saturday 15 June
Group A: **England v Scotland**
(Wembley, 3.00 pm) BBC

Group B: **France v Spain**
(Elland Road, 6.00 pm) ITV

Sunday 16 June
Group C: **Russia v Germany** ....
(Old Trafford, 3.00 pm) ITV

Group D: **Croatia v Denmark** ....
(Hillsborough, 6.00 pm) BBC

Monday 17 June
Another free day

Tuesday 18 June
Group B: **France v Bulgaria** ....
(St James' Park, 4.30 pm) BBC

Group B: **Romania v Spain** ....
(Elland Road, 4.30 pm) BBC

Group A: **Scotland v Switzerland** ....
(Villa Park, 7.30 pm) ITV

Group A: **Holland v England** ....
(Wembley, 7.30 pm) ITV

Wednesday 19 June
Group D: **Croatia v Portugal** ....
(City Ground, 4.30 pm) ITV

Group D: **Turkey v Denmark** ....
(Hillsborough, 4.30 pm) ITV

Group C: **Russia v Czech Republic** ....
(Anfield, 7.30 pm) BBC

Group C: **Italy v Germany** ....
(Old Trafford, 7.30 pm) BBC

Thursday 20 and Friday 21 June
Totally spare days.

QUARTER-FINALS   Winners

Saturday 22 June

Winner Group A v Runner-up Group B

.... v ....
(Wembley, 3.00 pm)

Winner Group B v Runner-up Group A

.... v ....
(Anfield, 6.30 pm)

Sunday 23 June

Winner Group C v Runner-up Group D

.... v ....
(Old Trafford, 3.00 pm)

Winner Group D v Runner-up Group C

.... v ....
(Villa Park, 6.30 pm)

Monday 24 and Tuesday 25 June
Finding-something-to-do days.

SEMI-FINALS	**Winners**

Wednesday 26 June

Winner Anfield v Winner Villa Park

.... v ....

(Old Trafford, 5.00 pm)

Winner Wembley v Winner Old Trafford

.... v ....

(Wembley, 7.30 pm)

Thursday 27 to Saturday 29 June
Looking-forward-to-the-final days.

FINAL	**Winners**

Sunday 30 June

.... v ....

(Wembley, 7.00pm) ITV and BBC

COUNTDOWN TO THE FINAL

Grab a biro and write in, as neatly as you can, the result of each match for your complete record of the 1996 tournament. No spider writing.

GROUP STAGE MATCHES: GROUP A
England, Switzerland, Holland, Scotland

Venues:
Wembley, London; Villa Park, Birmingham

Saturday 8 June, 3.00 pm; Wembley ITV
England v Switzerland
Score:

....

Goalscorers:

....

....

Monday 10 June, 4.30 pm; Villa Park ITV
Holland v Scotland
Score:

....

Goalscorers:

....

....

Thursday 13 June, 7.30 pm; Villa Park BBC
Switzerland v Holland
Score:

....

Goalscorers:

....

....

Saturday 15 June, 3.00 pm; Wembley BBC
England v Scotland
Score:

....

Goalscorers:

....

....

Tuesday 18 June, 7.30 pm; Villa Park ITV
Scotland v Switzerland
Score:

....

Goalscorers:

....

....

Tuesday 18 June, 7.30 pm; Wembley ITV
England v Holland
Score:

....

Goalscorers:

....

....

GROUP A FINAL TABLE

TEAM	P	W	D	L	F	A	G/D	PTS
A1								
A2								
A3								
A4								

GROUP STAGE MATCHES: GROUP B
Spain, Bulgaria, Romania, France

Venues:
Elland Road, Leeds; St James' Park, Newcastle

Sunday 9 June, 2.30 pm; Elland Road ITV
Spain v Bulgaria
Score:

....

Goalscorers:

....

....

Monday 10 June, 7.30 pm; St James' Park BBC
Romania v France
Score:

....

Goalscorers:

....

....

Thursday 13 June, 4.30 pm; St James' Park ITV
Bulgaria v Romania
Score:

....

Goalscorers:

....

....

Saturday 15 June, 6.00 pm; Elland Road ITV
France v Spain
Score:

....

Goalscorers:

....

....

Tuesday 18 June, 4.30 pm; St James' Park BBC
France v Bulgaria
Score:

....

Goalscorers:

....

....

Tuesday 18 June, 4.30 pm; Elland Road BBC
Romania v Spain
Score:

....

Goalscorers:

....

....

GROUP B FINAL TABLE

TEAM	P	W	D	L	F	A	G/D	PTS
B1								
B2								
B3								
B4								

GROUP STAGE MATCHES: GROUP C
Germany, Czech Republic, Italy, Russia

Venues:
Old Trafford, Manchester; Anfield, Liverpool

Sunday 9 June, 5.00 pm; Old Trafford BBC
Germany v Czech Republic
Score:

....

Goalscorers:

....

....

Tuesday 11 June, 4.30 pm; Anfield BBC
Italy v Russia
Score:

....

Goalscorers:

....

....

Friday 14 June, 7.30 pm; Anfield ITV
Czech Republic v Italy
Score:

....

Goalscorers:

....

....

Sunday 16 June, 3.00 pm, Old Trafford ITV
Russia v Germany
Score:

....

Goalscorers:

....

....

Wednesday 19 June, 7.30 pm; Anfield BBC
Russia v Czech Republic
Score:

....

Goalscorers:

....

....

Wednesday 19 June, 7.30 pm; Old Trafford BBC
Italy v Germany
Score:

....

Goalscorers:

....

....

GROUP C FINAL TABLE

TEAM	P	W	D	L	F	A	G/D	PTS
C1								
C2								
C3								
C4								

GROUP STAGE MATCHES: GROUP D
Denmark, Portugal, Turkey, Croatia

Venues:
Hillsborough, Sheffield; City Ground, Nottingham

Sunday 9 June, 7.30 pm; Hillsborough BBC
Denmark v Portugal
Score:

....

Goalscorers:

....

....

Tuesday 11 June, 7.30 pm; City Ground ITV
Turkey v Croatia
Score:

....

Goalscorers:

....

....

Friday 14 June, 4.30; City Ground BBC
Portugal v Turkey
Score:

....

Goalscorers:

....

....

Sunday 16 June, 6.00 pm; Hillsborough BBC
Croatia v Denmark
Score:

....

Goalscorers:

....

....

Wednesday 19 June, 4.30 pm; City Ground ITV
Croatia v Portugal
Score:

....

Goalscorers:

....

....

Wednesday 19 June, 4.30 pm; Hillsborough ITV
Turkey v Denmark
Score:

....

Goalscorers:

....

....

GROUP D FINAL TABLE

TEAM	P	W	D	L	F	A	G/D	PTS
D1								
D2								
D3								
D4								

QUARTER-FINALS

Saturday 22 June, 3.00 pm; Wembley
Winner Group A v Runner-up Group B

.... v ....
Score:

....
Goalscorers:

....
....

Saturday 22 June, 6.30 pm; Anfield
Winner Group B v Runner-up Group A

.... v ....
Score:

....
Goalscorers:

....
....

Sunday 23 June, 3.00 pm; Old Trafford
Winner Group C v Runner-up Group D

.... v ....
Score:

....
Goalscorers:

....
....

Sunday 23 June, 6.30 pm; Villa Park
Winner Group D v Runner-up Group C

.... v ....
Score:

....

Goalscorers:

....

....

SEMI-FINALS

Wednesday 26 June, 5.00 pm; Old Trafford
Winner Anfield v Winner Villa Park

.... v ....
Score:

....

Goalscorers:

....

....

Wednesday 26 June, 7.30 pm; Wembley
Winner Wembley v Winner Old Trafford

.... v ....
Score:

....

Goalscorers:

....

....

FINAL

Sunday 30 June, 7.00 pm; Wembley

.... v ....
Score:

....
Goalscorers:

....

....

Champions:

....

Verdict:

....

Match of the tournament:

....

Player of the tournament:

....

Best moment:

....

Worst moment:

....

Top goalscorer:

....